WOMEN WORKERS OF TEA PLANTATIONS IN INDIA

WOMEN WORKERS OF TEA PLANTATIONS IN INDIA

MITA BHADRA

HERITAGE

HERITAGE PUBLISHERS

NEW DELHI

INDIA 1992

Published in India 1992 by
HERITAGE PUBLISHERS
4, C Ansari Road
New Delhi-110002

ISBN-81-7026-172-4

Published by B.R. Chawla, for Heritage Publishers, 4-C, Ansari Road, New Delhi-110002 and printed at Efficient offset Printers, 215, Shahzada Bagh Indl. Complex, Delhi-110035, Laser Typeset by Mac Printec, 84 Darya Ganj, New Delhi.

DEDICATED TO
MY
MOTHER

Preface

It has been felt that there is a need for empirical research in the field of industrial sociology of women. The role of woman workers in industry, their adjustment to industrial environment, their attitudes and behaviour, commitment to work, pattern of promotions and their relationships with the employer as well as other employees have not yet been dealt with proper attention.

The 'Women Liberation Year' in 1975 has attracted a number of sociologists and social Anthropologists to study women from various perspectives. The researches on women concentrate mainly on the changing life and status of the middle class educated working women. Hardly there has been any effort to study the backward class woman workers. There are very few studies on women of the lower strata of our society, and there is in particular, no study available on the tea plantation woman workers of our country.

The main purpose of this study is to investigate the factors responsible for entering the plantation women in the labour force and the effect of employment on their socio-cultural life. The tea plantation has a distinct form of productive organisation which gives rise to certain specific social relations. In this study emphasis is given on role of woman workers in the productive process of tea plantation system, their life and work outside the family in employment and their life and work within the household and the process of adaptation and adjustment. Tea plantation is the only industry where employment is on family basis with a history of imported tribal labourers from faraway places who settled down with the confines of tea plantation. The system of labour recruitment on the family basis has made the women to seek employment obligatory and woman workers have a definite function to perform in tea industry as it is agro-based. Practically in some field-operations women are more suitable than men. The entire labour force is residential and the women can take up employment in tea plantation without causing serious disruption in their domestic life. Tea plantation has also a distinct form of social organisation which gives rise to certain specific form of social relations.

The status of women in tea plantation society depends upon the complexity of roles which they perform in socio-economic, cultural, religious and political spheres. The economic role that the plantation women perform as wage labourers has some special significance for understanding their position in the society. The multi-ethnic tribal woman workers of tea plantations of Terai region enjoy much more social freedom befitting their traditional tribal ethos. Their participation in plantation work does not adversely affect the inter-personal relationships among the family members. It does not create situation of conflict in the family. At the sametime the family members consider women's taking up out-of-home job as something natural in tune with the traditional tribal ethos. Though economic participation is very high among the women of tea plantations but their political participation is very low. Their educational attainment is also very very low and most of them are unskilled and organisationally unsophisticated. Though apparently the plantation woman workers enjoy considerable freedom still their overall position in society has remained low. The inequality between the men and the women extends in almost every sphere of life, in unequal wage rate, unauthorised deduction, unequal occupational status, unequal status in social, political and educational spheres. In the patriarchal plantation society there is no special identity for women. The patriarchal family system along with inferior educational standard, economic position and power position of women are the sources of inequality among men and women in plantation society. It is evident that women plantation workers have not witnessed significant changes in their life style over the years. Their ignorance, lack of skill and assertive nature make them subservient both at the place of work and in the family life.

Without the enthusiasm and cooperation of the woman workers of Chandmoni tea estate this study could not have been conducted. I am grateful to them as I am to the University Grants Commission for awarding me a Junior Research Fellowship and Senior

Research Fellowship. The book is a revised version of my doctoral thesis submitted to the University of North Bengal. I am also grateful to the authorities of the University of North Bengal for providing me the necessary facilities to carry out the research. I am thankful to Shri Aurobindo Ghosh, the then Manager of Chandmoni tea estate who allowed me to work freely among the woman labourers and to go through the official records. It would not have been possible for me to conduct my research work without his help. My thanks are also to Shri Gondra Munda, a worker of Chandmoni tea estate for his constant help and assistance. My husband Prof. Ranajit Kumar Bhadra devoted his valuable time in going through the manuscript. Obviously he does not need any special mention. I am also thankful to Dr. Sekh Rahim Mondal for his encouragement for publication of this book. My thanks are also due to Shri Jayanta Ghosh who has typed my manuscript in record time.

Finally I thankfully acknowledge the acceptance of Heritage Publishers, New Delhi to publish this book.

MITA BHADRA

University of North Bengal,
Raja Rammohanpur, Dist. Darjeeling,
West Bengal, 1991

Contents

Chapter 1

Introduction

The study sets out to examine the nature and work situation of the women workers of tea plantations of West Bengal. It aims to analyse the life and labour of these women workers. The main focus here is to delineate the nature of women's work participation in the tea industry and its consequent effect on their home life. It intends to analyse the various forces which shape the position in which the plantation women find themselves. Such forces have been changing over time. This study also reflects the changes in the status and roles of women employed in tea industry. It is quite evident that the position of women workers or the position of plantation labourers in general, could not be appreciated without a clear understanding of their nature of work and its organizational setting and its impact over their community life. There are certain features of tea plantation workers of West Bengal which distinguish them from the workers of the organised sector in other parts of India. Tea is a labour-intensive industry where half of the workforce consists of women workers.

A crucial part of tea plantations is its labour organisation. As a response to the manpower needs of the nineteenth century the planters of West Bengal and Assam deliberately collected labourers from outside the state and thus created an immigrant enclave community using their traditional social structure as a means of control. Almost all the workers engaged in tea plantations are immigrants or their descendants who have been recruited either from Chotanagpur and Santal Pargana regions of Bihar or Chattisgarh region of Madhya Pradesh and Orissa. They were mostly of tribal origin. Many of the principal structural features of the tea plantation society had their roots in the early slave plantation which had emerged due to the particular economic need and since then they had become the intrinsic part of the plantation system in general. The bulk of the labour consists of Oraon, Munda, Santal, Nagesia, Ho, Asur, Kheria, Ghasi, Baraik, Gond, Mahali, Turi and other tribal communities. To some extent West Bengal plantations employed migrant labourers from Nepal but this was by no means the major part of the labour populations. At present in Terai and Dooars plantations of West Bengal the Nepalese and other castes communities constitute only 15 per cent of the labour force and in Darjeeling hill plantations 85 per cent of the labour force is consisted of the Nepali migrants. The wider social background of plantation labour force of West Bengal was and still is of considerable importance for analysing their work participation and social structure. This study sets out to examine the nature and situation of women labourers in West Bengal tea plantations. The situation of women tea plantation workers of West Bengal reflects a phenomenon prevalent in varying degrees in most societies—male domination and discrimination against women. This is inevitably reflected in many aspects of the society particularly in the organisation of work and trade unions. Special attention is to be paid to women workers of tea plantations because their problems are always peculiar to them. Comparatively speaking they are much less organised. They also suffer from certain social prejudices and physical disabilities. That women are comparatively less suited for heavy work and are most vulnerable to situations in industry which produce fatigue are used as arguments to justify views which are often held in support of lower wages for women workers. They are either given lower jobs or the jobs which they handle traditionally become women's job carrying lower salaries. However since 1976 growing attention is being paid to reducing such inequality at different levels. Though it is not very significant. The principle for equal pay for equal work needs to be more vigourously implemented and the tendency to scale down the work in tea industry which is generally handled by women workers has to be guarded against. Training facilities and education should be provided for them so that they can compete for higher jobs. In addition the possibility of increasing opportunities for their part time employment should be explored. The specificity of plantation women's situation and their problems have certainly not been adequately dealt with.

Women labour is very often analysed using a framework that divides the world into two spheres of activities such as "production" and "reproduction". Productive activities are often associated with wage labour, while reproductive activities often deal with the world of cultural or even "natural" functions, i.e. the natural aspects of women for their existence. This study will try to interrelate between the different activities of women in production as well as at home. Before going into the details of the frame of this study it would be in order to present a brief review of the studies on women which, although limited, may serve to develop the rationale for this study.

Since the sixties although a good number of studies have been done on women anthropological dimension, however, has remained virtually neglected. These studies have mainly highlighted historical, economic, political and psychological dimensions of women's role in society. However, the subject matters remain confined to the women in economic and political activities, history of ideology of domesticity, liberation of women, etc. Inevitably, aims of these studies are concerned with the nature of women's oppression, their pains and problems, etc.

The "Women Liberation Year" in 1975 attracted a number of social anthropologists and sociologists to study women with various perspectives. All these studies reveal three different interpretations of women, and they can be grouped under three broad approaches, namely, Marxist, functionalist and feminist. According to the Marxists the position of women will vary from society to society and time to time according to the prevailing economic and political relationships. The Marxists place women in the modes of production of a society and interpret them forming a class which is subordinate to and oppressed by the superior class formed only by men under certain historical circumstances. At the same time they put little emphasis on the status differences between men and women. The Marxists consider the genesis of female subordination in the growing phenomenon of private property which, in their view, has made possible and necessary the exploitation of the biological differences. On the other hand, the functionalists are of the view that female activity in the home is essentially cultural. Their view has often been associated with a denial of the proposition that women do in fact constitute a subordinate group at all. Strictly speaking there is no theory of sex-linked stratification in functionalism. The feminists are however of the opinion that the system of male domination and female subjugation in the society arises essentially from biological inequality of sex. They believe that the biological inequality of man and woman provides the basis of the social institutions, particularly the family, which have developed to keep women oppressed. The feminists are much more concerned with the socio-economic oppression, exploitation and the liberation of women. There are two basic ideas which have emerged from the feminists' thought — one is egalitarianism and the other is liberationism. The first idea develops for the elimination of institutionally structured sex differences and sex roles. The second idea is based on the belief that the social institutions that oppress women as women also oppress people as people. In the following sections we will make a brief review of the earlier studies made on women from these three perspectives.

Women Studies : the Marxist Perspective

The importance of the position of women in human history and their role in social change are mentioned in the writings of Marx and Engels. In the theory of evolution of class society they have analysed women's role in social production and their relations to the development of family and private property. Marx has also pointed out the condition of women both in family and in wage labour when he has discussed on the nature and working of capitalism[1]. The form of family and the nature of women's oppression within it depend upon the particular type of class society to which it belongs. "The Origin of the Family, Private Property and the State" is more than an analysis of women's status. Set in an evolutionary framework, it shows how private property has originated, how the family has developed as an economic unit, how inequality of property ownership and finally exploitative class society have developed. It also shows how women's social position has declined as private property has gained strength. Engels has tried to establish the relationship between property, class and sex. Engels' idea about the public labour, private property and the family is very important for determining women's status. He presents a historical process by which women are transformed from free and equal productive members of society to subordinate and dependent wives and wards.[2] Marx and Engels have shared the view that the status of women in pre-class societies was much higher than the class societies which have developed later.

Classical Marxists argue that women are not an exploited group in the strict sense except in so far as they become wage labourers. Women are regarded as potential historical subjects only when they enter into the industrial labour force. It is argued by the classical Marxists that domestic labour does not produce surplus value. Since women as housewives and mothers are excluded from social production for the market, their subordination is not a constituent element of the class system in capitalist societies. Classical Marxists view that female emancipation must depend on the entry of women into social production[3]. Emphasis is now laid on how family functions to develop the capitalist order by the organized working class. Both the state and family may be seen as structures used to maintain and extend the class domination of property owners in order to control those who work but do not own. The Marxists view women as the proletariats.

The Marxist analysis of family under capitalism is twofold. One aspect is the role of the family in regulating property relations among the owners of the means of production. The other aspect deals with the part the family plays in the reproduction—both physical and social—and maintenance of wage labourers, the producers of wealth. The contradictory nature of capitalism lies in the fact that while industrial production is social, the ownership and control of property are increasingly concentrated in the private hands. Another contradictory aspect is that while production is social, the reproduction and daily maintenance of the work force is the private responsibility of each nuclear family. From these structural features the basic condition of the majority of women under capitalism is derived.[4]

Larguia explains the discrimination against women as the result of a hidden economic structure inherent to class society which can be defined in relation to the way in which surplus labour is extracted from class society. Larguia stated that class society is governed by two structural principles : (a) the division in the classes and (b) the family economic unit. The two structures are interdependent, and changes in one aspect bring changes in other. She further points out that the authoritarian nature of the family comes from the extraction of women's labour and the hidden economic activity within it absorbs half of human labour. Larguia considers that the unrecognized extraction of unskilled labour and the necessity of prolonging it is the basis for discrimination of women.[5] In a society where labour power is a commodity to be bought in the form of wages, women work to maintain the members of a family without being paid directly. Not only are women rendered economically dependent but their exploitation is often masked by the fact that their domestic work remains outside the commodity production.

Morton defines family as a unit whose function is maintenance and reproduction of labour power, i.e., the structure of the family is determined by the economic system for a certain kind of labour power at a particular time.[6] Following Morton's view Secombe and other Marxist–feminists have tried to establish the relationship between the wage labour and domestic labour. Thus she has elaborated Marx's formulation that the value of labour power is not only the value of subsistence necessary for the labourers but also include means necessary for the maintenance of the labourers and his substitutes, i.e., his children. She also tries to establish the relationship between the wage labour of women and their domestic labour. She formulates that married women enter into market place greater in number because the wage for their labour power is greater than the value that they can produce through domestic labour.[7] This analysis of the role of domestic labour, women's wage labour and the relationship between the two in capitalist society have been an important dimension in the Marxist theoretical understanding of women. It has also made important strides over the study of women from Marx–Engels' historical perspective.

Hamilton makes a thorough attempt to study the changing role of women in seventeenth century Europe from Marxist historical perspective. She examines how the rise of capitalism and the gradual acceptance of Protestantism have separately and together radically altered every aspect of women's life. She tries to work out the changes through a Marxist explanation and the deep rooted patriarchal ideology behind this transformation through a feminist explanation.[8]

The family and women's role in it also make women a labour reserve. They are hired depending upon the needs of the economy. The position of working class women is characteristic of relations between the sexes throughout the society. The relation between men and women is always embodied in the capitalist mode of production. Even in the middle class family man is the bourgeois and the wife represents the proletariat.[9]

Firestone has made a comprehensive statement that the fundamental biological inequality has given rise to the caste like system in which men dominate over women. Thus the two sexes have hierarchical relationship. This institutionalised inequality is the basis of women's oppression. She emphasizes that the achievement of full self-determination including economic independence of both women and children would require fundamental changes in our social and economic structure. Firestone's work is not dialectical because the notion of class contradiction is absent in her writing and the social universe is irreversibly split into two separate worlds, namely, material and cultural. It is a combination of crude materialism and ecological determinism but the class dialectic based on sex is not established in her writings.[10] Mitchell has criticized Firestone's attempt to incorporate Marxism within the "Radical Feminist" framework and advocates the search for a Marxist solution to the problems raised by the feminists. She further recommends a separate and independent analysis of structures of female oppression in different areas and in different societies and formulates to separate the conscious opposition from the unconscious opposition of women. According to her feminism is a conscious political ideology which arises in particular historical circumstances. Mitchell uses psychoanalysis for studying the classes and the position of women in human society. On the basis of Freudian findings, she has developed a theoretical analysis of patriarchy as a parallel theoretical analysis to her work on women and class. She emphasises that the capitalist mode of production and the ideological mode of patriarchy must be analysed separately.[11]

Sack tries to examine Engels' ideas about the importance of public labour, private property and the family for determining women's status. She explains the exploitative nature of class societies and the relationship of property to class and sex and separates two sets of ideas : (1) the material bases of women's status — that social or public labour makes men or women adult citizens in the eyes of society and that men's ownership of private property establishes their dominance over women in the family and society and (2) those about the evolutionary aspect — that women's status has become solely subordinate and domestic with the development of male private property, production for exchange, and class society. However, she does not support the second idea. According to her there are two aspects of women's position — women as social adults and women as wives. The two can vary somewhat independently. In class societies the subordinate position of women not only is derived from domestic property relations but from the male public power which denies women's social status. To her the dichotomization of family and society is very strong in class society. This makes women responsible for production of private use value and makes men responsible for the production of exchange values. Wage work becomes an additional burden which in no way changes women's domestic work and responsibility.[12]

Rowbotham has made an attempt for synthesising Marxism and feminism as these two are complementary to each other. She considers Marxism as a revolutionary weapon for encountering the oppression of women and considers women's work as that of wage labourers and houseworkers.[13]

The Marxist analysis of women helps to understand how the modes of production determine the lives of women within the household both by defining the internal structure of it and by locating their position in the social system. The position of women is better understood through the analysis of modes of production and their place in the class structure. It is common that the exploitation of women in capitalist society flows from the class relations. At the same time Marxism recognizes the special oppression of women, its institutional and ideological supports. Marxism offers a theory of functions of sexist institution, ideology and behaviour in supporting and maintaining the social system. The status of women, their domestic and non-domestic roles as wage labourers and the nature of family are central to the materialist theory of human social evolution. The sexual antagonism is one of the major social conflicts that helps to hold the society together.

Women Studies : The Functionalist Perspective

The structure-functionalists try to analyse the interrelations between women's status and the nature of social system, and view the women's activities in home as essentially cultural. They often deny that women do in fact constitute a subordinate group. Women have one conceptual set of images which are moulded by value system. Likewise they have a set of images of men which are structured by the central value system. Durkheim and Levi-Strauss set up dichotomies between sacred and profane, and arbitrarily designate men as sacred and women as profane, or men as actors and women as acted upon objects. Such polarized view is challenged by Kaberry and Goodale. They focus on interaction between the quotidian and the ritual activities of Australian aborigines. They describe the crucially important economic role of aboriginal women and show how these determine the nature of the spiritual role of women, refuting the male view that women are excluded from the sacred state.[14] Malinowski states the division of labour by sex that the Australian aboriginal women are forced to do heavier work by the other (brutal) half of society and the relation of a husband to wife in its economic aspect is that of a master to its slave and according to him the husband has a definite 'over-right' over his wife.[15]

The functionalists' view is that women should be studied in terms of role, function and attributes and they should be treated as a social category. Mead thinks that there is hardly any sex-linked aptitude or abilities which are universally acknowledged. In all societies there are certain abilities and aptitudes which can be considered as typically male and other as typically female.[16]

In modern anthropology the functional theory of family also expresses sexist bias. According to persons functionalism perceives a harmonious division of labour within the family between instrumental and expressive functions. The instrumental function is performed by male, head of the household and the expressive function by wife-mother. He characterizes the woman's role in the family as "expressive" which means she provides warmth, security and emotional support. This is essential for effective socialization of the young. The tasks appropriate to the wife-mother are therefore those of pattern maintenance and integration. But pattern maintenance and integration also prove to be the major functions of the family as a whole, acting as a solidarity unit in the context of an always potentially non-solidaristic total society. This form of the wife-mother functions within the family, by the family itself in the wider social system, only serves to reinforce the identification of the women's role with that of the family. The Parsonian theory also states that the root of functions of the family and pre-eminently of the adult woman as the key personality in the internal family structure are those of socialization and the emotional stabilization of the adult personality.[17]

Freeman analyses that female oppression in a society is particularly embodied in two core concepts starting essentially from the traditional belief. The first is that men are more important, more significant, more valuable and more worthwhile than those of women because men are the primary bread winners in the family. From the value comes the attitude that a husband must earn more than his wife otherwise he suffers from a loss of personal status. Secondly, women survive to please and assist men. Their role is complementary to that of men. They should fulfill the natural "femine" functions. As they are different from men they should not compete with them. From this concept comes the attitude that women are dependent on men for everything and more particularly for their social identities which define the socially rewarded roles as wife, mother and mistress. Women cannot become equal to men without the destruction of the interdependent and mutually parasitic roles of male and female. Therefore, integration of sex roles and the equality of sexes will inevitably lead to some basic structural changes of society.[18]

In India studies on women are mainly influenced by structure-functionalism. This is perhaps due to the history of origin of the two disciplines — Sociology and Social Anthropology in this country which have been initially influenced by British functionalism. Most of the women studies have been done to examine the changing roles, attitudes and functions of family, and its consequences in marital adjustment particularly of the educated urban one. However, it is found that such studies rarely take care of comparative study of men and women in similar occupations.[19]

Srinivas has studied a number of factors related to the caste system which clearly affect the position of women in Hindu society. Among the low castes the relationship between men and women is more egalitarian than among the higher castes. The lower castes also try to raise their status through sanskritisation, the consequence of which is the lowering of the status of women and making them subordinate to men in moral, economic and ritual terms.[20]

According to Karve the system of caste, family structure, kinship and marriage affect the status of women in a fundamental way. There are a number of factors related to caste in India which clearly affect the position of women in society.[21]

The traditional attitudes and practices related to the position of women vary from region to region and within a region from caste to caste. The regional variation is more important than caste variation. As Kolenda points out, the incidence of bride-price, divorce and remarriage varies in practice from region to region, despite differences in the ideals among castes within one region.[22] The changing attitudes towards family and marriage provide an indicator of the changing position of women. It is assumed that the forces of modernization and urbanization lead to a decrease in the number of joint families. Whether or not a woman lives in a joint family may have important consequences for her position in society and the opportunities that are open to her.

Another interesting dimension regarding caste is the extent to which caste background affects women's self image and influences selection of a role model or reference group. Beteille also points out that there are a number of caste related factors which clearly affect the position of women in Indian society. He also observes that among the poor and low castes the relationship between men and women is more egalitarian than among the higher castes.[23]

Devaki Jain contrasts feminists who deny that biological differences can be rarely extended to aptitudes. In all societies there are certain abilities and aptitudes which are typically male and others are typically female. She argues that research formulations will depend upon whether women are considered similar to or different from men.[24]

The system of arranged marriages appears to be core of the society's ability to sustain traditional images and role for women, except the revolutionary changes in the economic and political spheres of a wider society. The complex interrelationship of regionalism, caste, religion and joint family is a condition specific to the situation of Indian women.[25]

Although marriage and kinship have been studied in relation to women in a society, recently scholars have taken interest in studying position of women, their changing role, status and attitudes.[26] Beliefs and practices regarding pollution have been widely studied as the scholars consider the concepts of female suspectability to pollution to be central to the structure of the whole society. In the ritual sphere there is a dichotomy between male and female activities and rarely they share an equal ritual role.[27]

Recently a good number of studies have been done on working women in India. These studies have concentrated on the changing status of middle class women and consequent problems of their marital adjustment.[28] Kapur has studied the middle class educated urban working women for understanding their changing status, attitudes, marital and familial relationships. It is found that educated women workers are not only more tolerated and accepted in the society than before, but are even more respected and admired. Old prejudices against work in offices and shops are gradually declining. Unmarried and married women of middle and upper classes are increasingly entering into all types of office jobs both in public and private sectors. Women are getting into jobs and professions and continue even after their marriage not only out of sheer economic necessity but also out of various other socio-psycho-situational factors and motivation. Kapur explores the various factors affecting the marital adjustment of the middle class working women. The multiple factors studied are objective and subjective.

The objective factors are the family composition, husband's income, number of dependents, types of wife's service and husband's occupation. The subjective factors are the agreement or disagreement between husband and wife on values of life, each other's role and status, sharing of household responsibilities, etc.[29] According to Srivastava, the educated urban women work mainly for certain non-economic advantages. Employment has raised the status of educated middle class women and they have become more conscious and independent. As both husband and wife co-operate and share domestic responsibilities there is not much problem in functioning of the family. Therefore, women's participation in work does not adversely affect the interpersonal relationship between husband and wife, and also the authority structure of the family. It is observed that working women belonging to the lower class groups, however, are not much in favour of women's employment, they face much difficulties to work both in home and outside. The educated employed women are favourably oriented towards freedom from traditionality. It is found that education and employment act as determinants of modernity.[30]

Women Studies : The Feminist Perspective

The feminists define the system of male domination and female subjugation in society and try to assert the position of women in sexual hierarchy. Women as housewives as well as mothers have some cultural functions which are often determined through the sex-based ideology of inequality. The feminists critiques start from the premises that differ completely from the traditional view of society. The feminist approach is completely different from the structural-functional approach of women study. The feminists consider that men and women are constitutionally equal and share the same human capabilities. Observed differences therefore demand a critical analysis of the social institutions that cause them. The analysis has been able to account for the differences in life chances between men and women in society, but there is a lack of differences among women. The whole theoretical edifice is founded on the concept of "patriarchy" which is a universal system of political domination functioning with the realm of sex relationships. For the feminists the position of women is the question and issue and beginning. The twentieth-century feminism made its contribution to the women's movement.

Firestone has made the most comprehensive statement on feminism. She states that there is a caste like system of stratification upon the biological inequality of sexes. In such inequality men receive the ego gratification and enjoy creature comforts from their domination on women. Central to the analysis was the family. She insists that the achievement of full self-determination including economic independence to both women and children would require fundamental changes in our social and economic structure.[31]

The central theoretical orientation of Millett's study is based on the concept of "patriarchy". She argues that female has fewer permanent class association than male. Women form a dependent class who live on surplus and their very existence is parasitic on men who rule them.[32] Millett contradicts herself on this point as she earlier points out that the pre-eminent arena of sexual revolution is within the consciousness itself.

Radical feminism has brought out a very important truth but it is a general non-specific truth.[33] The feminist approach lacks a particular analysis of the social relations of production. There is a lack of use of the method of history and psychoanalysis in its theory. The individual history, how a man or woman is made in social terms, how the biological differences are transformed into their social meanings, etc. have not been considered in the feminist approach. This approach is more concerned with asserting equal rights for both the sexes. In this sense it is more a socio-political movement than an effort to theorize the status of women.

So far, the approaches to the study of women, namely, the Marxist, the functionalist and the feminist have been discussed. The functionalist approach seeks to understand the place of women in the total social system. Such an analysis generally provides cultural interpretation of women in society. The feminist approach is much more concerned with the female oppression and their liberation having a political overtone. The Marxists interpret the structural location of women in capitalist society. At first, Marxist analysis concentrated mainly upon a discussion of the articulation between domestic labour and capitalism, but more recently there has been a hightened interest in the role of female wage labour as a variant of the industrial reserve army. Contributors of both fields have urged that it is necessary to examine the inter-relationships between patriarchy and capitalism if one is to develop an adequate theory of the sources of female subordination. The problem that is specific to the field of women studies is the female factors and female awareness. The female factors, e.g., women's complementarity to men, their conceptual positioning originate in a particular category of social relationship which generates from the culturally defined images held by one sex to another. The anthropological significance of the female factors lies in the extent to which it determines the socio-economic and cultural structure of the society.

THE NEED FOR INDUSTRIAL ANTHROPOLOGY OF WOMEN : THE PROBLEM OF THE STUDY

It is revealed from the foregoing discussion on the approaches to the study of women that only the Marxist approach has shown a keen interest to look at the position of industrial women in the capitalist society. The studies made on women from various perspectives like their status and roles in the society, employment in new profession, their position, etc. have considerably ignored to study the women who constitute an important part of industrial work force. Even in anthropology study of industrial women has been neglected. The study of industry would ideally cover all studies dealing with the production system or systems obtaining in a society in relation to one or more aspects of the total social system.[34] It is true that production system of a society not only includes male workers but also women workers either directly or indirectly, either partially or wholly along with the other aspects of the system.

However, the study of women industrial workers has remained an unexplored area. Specific studies bearing upon the problems of industrial women are almost rare. An anthropology of industrial occupations which concentrates solely on the male workforce leads to a neglect of an important source of differentiation within the workforce as a whole. The area of study in which a total neglect is noticed is the plantation industry. Women plantation workers appear as the most neglected category in anthropology despite the fact that they constitute a numerical majority of the industrial employees in the organised sectors of industry in India. However, we will deal with this aspect in some details in the next chapter.

A good number of scholars have already worked in the field of anthropology of industry. But most of them have not shown much interest in the study of industrial women workers. Most of these studies examine specific factory population in developing countries. To Kerr, socio-economic development involves conflict between traditional and modern ways of life which can restrain the pace of development and has important implications for the development of industrial labour force. The worker is uprooted from the larger family and village. The immediate family at least for a period is left in the village. These dislocations are accompanied frequently with a new position and status for women, many of whom may also come to be wage workers in factories or service employment.[35]

To Moore, the workers in an advanced industrial society are expected to show better adjustment, reflect greater occupational and geographical mobility and possess a higher level of commitment than in a less developed society.[36]

Nash has demonstrated a co-existence between workers' allegiance to the factory and their commitments to their traditional social structure in a Guatemalan factory.[37]

Lambert has found that the impact of technology varies according to the relative distance of the production system of a given factory from the traditional technology of the people.[38]

Morris shows that the shift from traditional, rural, agricultural occupations to modern, urban, industrial occupations has not been difficult. He has suggested that there has never been a real shortage of labour in Bombay, and whenever job opportunities are available people have moved from near as well as distant parts of the country. In the factory situation, it appears that the language, the region and religion are more important criteria than the caste, to make distinction within the work force.[39]

Sheth has studied the formal, informal and cultural relationship among the people in a factory. He emphasises the migratory status of the workers. He argues that the culture and values of a pre-industrial society often co-exist with those attributed to the industrial society, producing an inter-mixture of traditionalistic and rationalistic norms.[40]

Sharma examines the problem of recruitment of workers to industrial jobs and their commitment to industry as well as the industrial ways of life.[41]

Ramaswamy has studied employees' involvement in trade union activity in the context of their economic and political affiliations, work situations, the network of social relationships woven into trade union organization and employers' behaviour and attitudes.[42]

Bhowmik has studied the class formation among plantation workers in West Bengal. He has seen the relation between the planter and worker as that of 'master and servant' and not of 'employer and employee'. The labourers had few routes of escape and they were forced into accepting the conditions of life and work imposed on them by the plantation. He has traced the growth of the trade union movement among the plantation industrial workers in West Bengal with special reference to a particular garden in Dooars.[43]

Apart from the above general studies there are a few studies exclusively on industrial women. There is a general neglect to consider women work participation in the labour market separately. However, the increasing work participation of women in industry has some anthropological significance.

Piho has studied life and labour of women textile workers in Mexico city. Her study deals with the life of the Mexican women workers in general, and with the life of the textile women workers in particular. The study concerns with the working conditions, income, relationships with other workers in the factory, living conditions at home, main problems, role in the family, etc. This study investigates the real economic and social situation of women textile workers in Mexico city. The findings show that the use of the working woman's income is directly related to the number of family members depending on her, although some of them help to pay the common costs of living for the whole family group. The working woman is used to a certain personal freedom and therefore is willing to maintain her working status as long as possible.[44]

In her study on Puerto Rican woman Silvestrini-Pacheco shows that the development of the tobacco-growing industry and the rise of the needle-work industry have a considerable effect on the status of women because they help to incorporate large number of women as workers. Previously women had participated indirectly in agricultural activities such as sugar and coffee production, and their role was less important than that of the male workers. But both in the tobacco processing and needle-work industries women constituted a significant portion of the labour force and were directly responsible for the elaboration of the end products. Thus they had the opportunity to participate actively, together with male workers, in the labour struggle in the 1930's. Pacheco shows how the Puerto Rican women have raised their level of awareness and increased their collaboration with other social movements. After the strike in 1933, the women needed labour unions responsive to their social problems and thus began organizing their own labour groups. By their efforts the Puerto Rican women workers had begun a new chapter in the social history of Puerto Rico. Women's work and their participation in the economy of Puerto Rico certainly facilitated their engagement in political and social struggle of the island. Gradually, women also have become active in the pro-independence movement and in other political activities.[45]

Nash has studied women in Bolivian tin-mining communities. The special nature of the mining community cultivates a total participation of all those who live and work in it; in part because of the isolation and in part because everyone is directly or indirectly dependent on the same enterprise. The rate of pay directly affects men, women, and children. Men and women have joined together in economic and political actions to demand improvement. Mining women are not isolated from each other or from the scene of industrial struggle because the encampment is an extension of the industrial complex itself. As active participants in the work process, the women have developed their own organizations to defend their rights as workers. Women's entry into the resistance movement signals the breakdown not only of a normal social structure, but also of the personal relationships that underlie it. Thus women's struggle of the Bolivian tin mining communities hightens the sense of social breakdown and shakes the very foundation of the dominant-subordinate hierarchy which has its roots in the home and family networks.[46]

Boserup explains the low rates of female employment in industry. Often the women tend to prefer work in home industries or in service trades rather than in wage employment in large-scale industries. The more flexible working hours in home industries are of great advantage to married women, and particularly to women with small children. It is possible to obtain part-time employment in home industries but impossible or at least difficult in large industries with a more rigorous rhythm of works. A manpower survey in Philippines shows that among self-employed women in home industries and women who are helping in family industries, i.e. among those who could decide more or less freely their own working hours, only 36-38 per cent work about 40 hours or more per weak, while 68 per cent of women wage workers in industry work about 40 hours or more per week. In Indonesia, modern industries attract women workers by offering part time employment. An official report of Calcutta suggests that a similar arrangement in the factories might be a suitable method to attract middle class women to industrial employment.[47]

It is however revealed from the history and development of anthropology both in the West and particularly in India that role of women workers has been neglected in the anthropological study of industrial system. In the beginning, social scientists working on industrial problems were guided by two somewhat incompatible tasks : (i) concern with the industrial efficiency and productivity and (ii) concern with the basic democratic values of equality and justice. The scholars felt committed to the dual goals of productivity and social equality. The question of social equality in the industrial system has however remained somewhat vague to the scholars. They could not deal with the problem of social equality with totality of the system because of their sexist bias. While the women labour force is an important part of the total labour force their problems and inequality have not been considered in any anthropological study of industry. Most of the anthropological study of industry interpret their work behaviour in a simplistic manner. The position of women in the class structure, the role of women in the capitalist mode of production and structural inequality have often been neglected. Such neglect of women in industrial occupations cannot be usefully accounted simply in terms of a sexist orientation. It is possible to speculate that the general neglect is due to the fact that the anthropologists rarely offer any insight to study the women workers in industry. Many of them believe that women are mere transients in the labour force and they have no serious role in industry and no serious commitment to collective organisation. But in all industrial societies women are increasingly entering in the labour force. Such increasing work participation of women in industry has some anthropological significance. When women take work in industry along with men, what is its impact on them and changes in their lives, i.e., status, prestige, responsibilities, roles, relations with others, kinship ties, etc. which might have altered considerably. A wide range of social system can be examined, i.e., family, workgroup, union, friendship network, neighbourhood, community, etc. in terms of anthropology of industry. The study of industrial women will open an avenue in the study of anthropology. The study of industrial women should be linked to the analysis of the total social structure and the role of women in this particular structure.

The present study will try to fill up some of the gaps in the field of industrial women particularly concerning with the problems of women workers of tea plantation industry in West Bengal. The female work participation in tea industry in West Bengal as well as in India is much higher than in any other industry. Tea industry experienced a regular increase of female labour since its establishment. West Bengal provides the largest chunk of non-agricultural female workers (being 19 per cent) of which almost 80 per cent are labourers in tea plantations.[48]

Plantation system has a social system with distinct class structure, economy and ways of life that separate it from the rest of the industrial society. The plantation is an organised industrial sector where men are the privileged group while to be women means to have a series of limitations. The problems which plantation women workers face have a specific colouring depending upon their socio-economic and cultural milieu in which they have been nurtured and moulded. There are certain limitations for them both in the working situation and in the family situation. Then what are such limitations? Where do plantation women stand in their traditional social structure? In order to analyse the status of an exploited group, this study deals with the major factors affecting the status of women workers in plantation.

The present study was conducted in Chandmoni Tea Estate in Darjeeling district of West Bengal. The tea plantation has a labour force of which 43 per cent are from the women workers while rest of the workers are men. Most of them belong to various tribal groups and a few are non-tribals the details of which has been given in Chapter 3. The purpose of this study is to analyse the role of women workers in the plantation, the nature of their work participation in the industry and the consequent adjustment in the home life. Tea industry is agro-based located in rural areas. The women workers, who have come mostly from villages of Bihar, Madhya Pradesh and Orissa can, therefore, be expected to be better adapted to this type of industry with a consequent effect upon lessening the conflict between home and work life. In the plantation in most of the cases both husbands and wives are employed, and they are subject to constraints of various challenges in the working place as well as in their home.

In this study particular emphasis will be given on the role of women in the productive process in the plantation industry, their life and work in the work situation and within the household. A thorough attempt has been made to analyse plantation women's role as wage labourers and housekeepers. It is felt that an understanding of their work, the conditions under which they work, the way they experience these and their problems would be a necessary precondition for further understanding of the problems of the plantation women workers.

This study concentrates on the following specific issues: the ethnic background of the women workers and their place in the rural society, their household composition, education, place of origin, process of recruitment, working facilities and prospects, income, etc. All these have some impact on their working life. The study concerns with the working conditions in the plantation and labourers' commitment to work, their relations with the management and the other workers of the plantation, the specific problems which the labourers face, their interactions with the outside world and common membership in a group, their kinship obligation, economic relations, trade union affiliation, etc.

Looking at the life of the plantation women workers two distinct aspects can be distinguished : the women workers at the work environment and at the home environment. The plantation women workers are mostly immigrated Adivasi people whose traditional occupation was agriculture. But in plantation they enter into the industrial working environment. Such changes have some important consequences upon the working life and home life of the workers. Therefore, it is necessary to know how far the Adivasi women have adjusted themselves to the industrial environment and what are their attitudes to the plantation work. Generally in plantation men and women perform different types of work. Naturally their wages also vary. Under such a situation then what is the inducement to work for both the sexes and what is the nature of their commitment to the industrial works? What is the role of women in the trade union activities? When the Adivasi women enter into the industrial work in plantation what impact is noticed in their social life? Is there any change of status of women workers due to their active economic participation? How far their roles have changed. If so, then how they have adjusted themselves in the home life and in the intra-family relations with other members. How they manage the home situation. What is the nature of their marital adjustment? In order to analyse the status of plantation women workers, this study deals with the major factors affecting the status of women workers in plantation.

This analytical study covers the following dimensions of the life of the plantation women workers:

(a) The women at the work situation — attitudes of women workers to their work; the nature of commitment; differential work performance by women of different ethnic groups, if any; duty or task of women workers vis-a-vis male workers; wage-structure of women vis-a-vis male workers; inducement to work of both male and female workers; women's role in trade union activities.

(b) The women at home — marital adjustment; husband's attitudes towards wives, employment; childcare and socialization of the children; management of home; economic contribution and sharing of household responsibilities; changing role and status of woman in the family, etc.

METHODOLOGY

The tea growing region of West Bengal is situated in the northern boundary consisting of two districts, namely, Jalpaiguri and Darjeeling. According to the Tea Statistics, 1978-79 there were 298 tea plantations in these two districts in 1977. In this year the total number of labour force in tea plantation was 205, 466 of which 96,255 were women labourers, 87,289 were men labourers, 8,0003 were adolescent and 13,919 were children. This working population is distributed among some major Adivasis and caste communication, namely, Oraon, Munda, Kharia, Nepali, etc. Besides there are a few minor communities like Mahali, Ghasi, Malpahari, Asur, Lohar, Turi, Ore, etc. All of them except the Nepalis are from Chotanagpur, Madhya Pradesh and Orissa regions. Only the Nepali (96 per cent) workers are found in the plantations on the Darjeeling hills. They are only 7 per cent in the plantations of the plain (Terai and Dooars) regions. Besides, a few local communities, namely, Mech, Rabha and Rajbansi are found as plantation labourers. However, in every plantation workers belong to most of these adivasis and caste communities. The management of the plantation of this region is more or less same except some minor differences found in the British owned plantations. The hierarchy in plantation, process of recruitment, wage pattern, job opportunities, etc. are also same in all the plantations. Due to these reasons it is thought that study of any plantation will be a representative one. Keeping this view in mind a tea plantation named Chandmoni Tea Estate is selected for the present study. Chandmoni Tea Estate is in Siliguri sub-division of Darjeeling district.

The data were collected from published materials and field study. For writing the 1st, 2nd and 3rd chapters considerable library work was done to go through the historical records, theoretical aspects of women studies, etc. Besides, relevant studies on women were also consulted. To obtain first hand data a field work of about ten months was conducted in Chandmoni Tea Estate during the period 1979-80. For the primary information a census enumeration schedule was used. Then an intensive interview was followed using an interview guide. As the total number of women workers was only 221 all of them were interviewed. Out of 221 only 14 belong to caste groups and rest are from various Adivasi communities. However, as the number of non-Adivasi women workers are very insignificant, we do not intend to make any comparative study between the Adivasi and caste women workers. Several case studies were conducted relating to the specific aspects of the life and labour of the women workers. The information collected through interview guide and case studies were supplemented by the data collected through observation. As the study concentrates upon the dual roles of women as plantation workers and housewives the respondents were mostly the married working women. However, in some cases unmarried women and widow workers were also interviewed. In several cases both husband and wife of same household were interviewed. All these interviews were supplemented with the interview of persons of resources who had a special knowledge of the community as well as industry. Most of the interviews took place in the informants' house and sometimes in the working place also. Besides, various records related to the women workers as well as men workers, such as pay, leave, absenteeism, turn-over, job opportunities and facilities, work rules, management, etc. were also collected from office of the Chandmoni Tea Estate. The data collected through all these sources are mostly qualitatively analysed.

References

1. Marx, Karl, *Capital*, Vol. 1, Progress Publishers, Moscow, 1971, pp. 372-379.
2. Engels, F., *The Origin of the Family, Private Property and the State*, Progress Publishers, Moscow, 1972.
3. Middleton, C., "Sexual inequality and Stratification Theory" in F. Parkin, (ed.), *The Social Analysis of Class Structure*, Tavistock Publications, London, 1974, pp. 186-187.
4. Schoepf, B.G. and Mariotti, A.M., "Politics of theory : Participant Observation in the United States" in R. Rohrlich-Leavitt (ed.), *Women Cross-Culturally*, Mouton Publishers, Hague, Paris, 1975, p. 393.
5. Larguia, L., "The Economic Basis of the Status of Women" in R. Rohrlich-Leavitt (ed.), ibid., pp. 281-282.
6. For details of female labour power in family as well as in society explained by P. Morton see R. Hamilton, *The Liberation of Women*, George Allen and Unwin, London, 1978, pp. 78, 86.
7. Secombe, W., "Domestic Labour — A Reply to Critics" in *New Left Review*, No. 94, 1975, p. 87.
8. Hamilton, R., op. cit.
9. Marx, K. and Engels, F., *Selected Works*, Lawrence & Wishart, London, 1986, p. 510.
10. For S. Firestone's "The Dialectic of Sex" see R. Hamilton, op.cit., pp. 84-87.
11. Mitchell, J., "Women and Equality" in J. Mitchell and A. Oakley (eds.), *The Rights and Wrongs of Women*, Penguin Books, England, 1976, p. 380.
12. Sacks, K., "Engels Revisited : Women, the Organization of Production, and Private Property" in R.R. Reiter (ed.), *Towards an An-*

thropology of Women, Monthly Review Press, New York & London, 1975, pp. 211-234.

13. Rowbotham, S., *Women's Consciousness – Man's World,* Pelican Books, Harmondsworth, England, 1973.
14. Rohrlich – Leavitt, R., B. Sykes, and E. Weatherford, "Aboriginal Woman : Male and Female Anthropological Perspectives" in R. Rohrlich-Leavitt (ed.), op.cit., pp. 570-71.
15. Ibid., pp. 571-572.
16. Mead, M., *Male and Female,* Dell Publishing Co., New York, 1948, pp. 288-289.
17. Parsons, T., *Essays in Sociological Theory,* Light and Life Publishers, New Delhi, 1975, pp. 69-88.
18. Freeman, J., "The Women's Liberation Movement in the United States" in R. Rohrlich-Leavitt (ed.), op cit., pp. 382-386.
19. Singh, A.M., "The Study of Women in South Asia : Some Current Methodological and Research Issues" in A. deSouza (ed.), *Women in Contemporary India and South Asia,* Manohar, New Delhi, 1980, p. 67.
20. Srinivas, M.N., *The Changing Position of Indian Women,* Oxford University Press, New Delhi, 1978, pp. 16-29.
21. Karve, 1., *Kinship Organisation in India,* Asia Publishing House, Bombay, 1965.
22. For P.M. Kolenda see A.M. Singh, "The Study of Women in India : Some Problems in Methodology" in A. deSouza (ed.), *Women in Contemporary India,* Manohar, New Delhi, 1975, pp. 194, 207.
23. Beteille, A., "The position of Women in Indian Society" in Devaki Jain (ed.), *Indian Women,* Ministry of Information and Broadcasting, Government of India, New Delhi, 1975.
24. Jain, Devaki (ed.), Ibid., p. XIII.
25. Singh, A.M., "The Study of Women in India : Some Problems in Methodology" in A. de Souza (ed.), *Women in Contemporary India,* Manohar, Delhi, 1975, p. 217.
26. Desai, N., *Women in Modern India,* Vora & Co. Publishers Pvt. Ltd., Bombay, 1957.

    Dube, S.C., "Men's and Women's Roles in India" in B.E. Ward (ed.) *Women in New Asia,* UNESCO, Paris, 1963.

    Hate, C.A., *Changing Status of Women in Post-Independence India,* Allied Publishers Pvt. Limited, Bombay, 1969.

    Kapadia, K.M., *Marriage and Family in India,* Oxford University Press, Bombay, 1958.
27. Singh, A.M., 1975 op.cit., pp. 203-204.
28. Kapur, P., *The Changing Status of Working Women in India,*

Vikas Publishing House, New Delhi, 1974. See also her, *Marriage and the Working Women in India,* Vikas Publishing House, New Delhi, 1970. Khanna, G. and M.A. Varghese, *Indian Women Today,* Vikas Publishing House, New Delhi, 1978.

Srivastava, V., *Employment of Educated Married Women in India,* National Publishing House, New Delhi, 1978.

29. Kapur, p., ibid., 1970.
30. Srivastava, V., op.cit.
31. For S. Firestone's "The Dialectric of Sex" see R. Hamilton, op.cit., pp. 84-89.
32. Millett, K., *Sexual Politics,* Hart Davis, London, 1971.
33. Mitchell, J., *Women's Estate,* Penguin Books, Harmondsworth, England, 1971, p. 90.
34. Sheth, N.R. and P.J. Patel, *Industrial Sociology in India,* Rawat Publications, Jaipur, 1979, p. 6.
35. Kerr, C., J.T. Dunlop, F.H. Harbison, and C.A. Myers, *Industrialism and Industrial Man,* Heinemann, London, 1962.
36. Moore, W.E., *Social Change,* Prentice Hall International INC, London, 1963.
37. Nash, M., *Machine Age Maya : The Industrialization in a Gautemalan Community,* American Anthropological Association, Memoir No. 87, 1958.
38. Lambert, R.D., *Workers Factories and Social Change in India,* Princeton University Press, Princeton NJ, 1963.
39. Morris, Morris, D., *The Emergence of an Industrial Labour Force: A Study of Bombay Cotton Mills 1854-1947,* Berkley, California, 1963.
40. Sheth, N.R., *The Social Framework of an Indian Factory,* (2nd edition), Hindustan Publishing Corporation, Delhi, 1981.
41. Sharma, B.R., *The Indian Industrial Workers,* Vikas Publishing House Pvt. Ltd., New Delhi, 1974.
42. Ramaswamy, E.A., *The Worker and His Union,* Allied Publishers, New Delhi, 1977.
43. Bhowmik, S., *Class Formation in the Plantation System,* Peoples Publishing House, New Delhi, 1981.
44. Piho, V., "Life and Labour of the Women Textile Workers in the Mexico City" in R. Rohelich-Leavitt (ed.), op. cit., pp. 199-246.
45. Silvestrini-Pacheco, B., "Women as Workers : The Experience of the Puerto Rican Woman in 1930's in R. Rohrlich-Leavitt (ed.), ibid., pp. 247-260.
46. Nash, J., "Resistance as Protest : Women in the Struggle of Bolivian Tin-Mining Communities" in R. Rohrlich-Leavitt (ed.), ibid., pp. 261-271.

47. Boserup. E., *Women's Role in Economic Development*, George Allen & Unwin, London, 1970, pp. 114-115.

48. Mitra, A., L.M. Pathak, and S. Mukherjee, *The Status of Women-Shifts in Occupational Participation, 1961-1971*, Abhinav Publications, New Delhi, 1980, p. 106.

Chapter 2

Women in the Working Force in India

The present chapter deals with the women's position in the working force in India in general and specifically in the plantation labour force. This will provide us with an answer to the question: why one should put his interests in the study of plantation women workers? In the organised sector of industry, Plantations occupy a unique position due to its agro-industrial features and highest percentage of women's employment. Women's employment situation in India differs from that of men. To study this situation it is essential to examine the sex-wise composition of the Indian labour force in terms of occupation, employment status and place of work. Between rural and urban areas, however, there are differences of occupational patterns.

The Trend of Women Labour Participation

Two distinguishable trends of women labour participation were noticeable in India. There was a specific set of livelihood categories in which women's participation rate declined steeply and linearly between 1901 and 1951. Also a second set of categories was found in which women work participation showed signs of improvement during the same period. In the total working force of women a constant decline had been noticed since the early part of this century (Table 1.) In 1901 the female work participation rate was 31.70 per cent and by 1951 it came down to 23.30 per cent. It has been observed from the census figures that the rate of women work participation varied from region to region, whereas in case of men it remained more or less constant. The proportion of women in agriculture showed an increase from 67 per cent in 1901 to 74 per cent in 1961. Employment outside agriculture indicated a steady fall from 23 per cent in 1901 to 13.7 per cent in 1961.[1] The number of women workers declined in food, textile, leather and ceramic industries over 1901-61 period. There were also a number of occupations and industries where women were being employed in increasing numbers and in which reservations for female employment were justified, e.g., teachers, nurses, community health workers, pediatricians, nutritionists, social education and welfare workers as well as a large range of blue and white collar workers in manufacturing, construction, trade and commerce, transport and service industries like accountants, book-keepers, secretaries and other professional workers. The 1961 census showed that there was an employment of women workers in large numbers in organised and unorganised sectors. During 1911-51 the number of women workers in the non-agricultural sector decreased by 2.5 million while that of men workers increased by 6.4 million. During 1951-61 there was an increase in the non-agricultural sector, 8.1 million for men but only 1.5 million for women. So

Table 1

Percentage Distribution of Women Workers in Various Occupations (1901-61)

Year	Female Working Population	Cultivators, Women Workers in Total	Agricultural Labourers	Mining, Plantation, etc.
1	2	3	4	5
1901	31.70	14.44	8.17	1.02
1911	33.73	14.73	10.34	1.17
1921	32.67	16.52	8.15	1.17
1931	27.63	8.95	11.02	1.16
1951	23.30	10.59	7.31	0.78
1961	27.96	15.59	6.67	0.56

Source: Census of India, 1961, paper No. 1 (p. 396). See also, Srivastava, V., *Employment of Educated Married Women in India,* National Publishing House New Delhi, 1978, p. 15.

Note: Workers here cover all categories of workers, viz., employers, employees, independent workers and family workers. Except in 1961, household industry was included in manufacturing and mining, etc. Percentage of workers to total female population regardless of age.

Table 1 (Contd.)

House-Hold Industry	Manufacturing Other than Household	Construction	Trade and Commerce	Transport, Storage and Communication	Other Services
6	7	8	9	10	11
—	3.95	0.21	1.87	1.03	1.95
—	3.54	0.24	1.83	0.06	1.95
—	3.01	0.24	1.78	0.05	1.75
—	2.41	0.21	1.41	0.04	2.43
—	1.62	0.17	0.66	0.07	2.10
2.20	0.37	0.11	0.38	0.03	2.05

far as the censuses of 1961 and 1971 were concerned the number of female workers per 10,000 males decreased from 4,606 to 2,099 in the agricultural sector and from 2,677 to 1,287 in non-agricultural activities during 1961-71. The decrease in work participation sex ratio was higher among non-agricultural workers but agricultural workers had also recorded a sharp fall.

In the capital intensive industrial sectors in India there was a limited employment generating capacity, the scope for employment of men workers had been limited but it had even more constricted for women workers. Women workers were mostly employed in labour intensive occupations like tea, coffee, rubber and coconut plantations, carpet weaving, laundry, bidi making or making of matches, coir making, construction work, poultery and kiln work and food processing activities.[2] The 1961 census showed that the number and proportion of women declined in food, textiles, leather and ceramics etc. over the 1901-61 period and that their extremely limited number in metallurgical, chemical and engineering groups indicated that women had failed to capture an adequate share of employment opportunities in major industries. This showed a trend of deindustrialization of female work force. In both cotton and jute industries the decline of women employment was attributed mainly to technological changes. It seemed that only agriculture had increased employment potentialities for women workers. In urban occupations education and medical services alone constituted areas of significantly expanding women's employment. But it was too low to make a marked impact on the overall participation of women in economic activities. The work participation rate of urban women was significantly lower than that of rural and the work participation rate of literate women was always lower than that of illiterate women.[3] The proportion of workers in low prestigious occupations was higher among women than among men.

Rural and Urban Occupational Structure

Women constitute nearly a third of the working force in India. In 1961, out of a total working force of 188.67 million, 59.5 million or 31.5 per cent were women. The great majority of women workers (55.4 million) lived in rural areas and worked in agriculture and allied occupations. In urban population there were 26.43 million workers — 22.42 million men and 4.01 million women. Women had increasingly been attracted to the jobs of industrial and non-industrial sectors which were formerly considered exclusively for men. The census data of 1961 showed that a great majority of women workers were engaged in agriculture, traditional rural industries and service occupations. In rural sectors there were 93.27 per cent women workers and in urban sectors there were only 6.73 per cent. The great majority of men workers (82.50 per cent) were also in rural areas, but the proportion was higher among the women (Table 2).[5]

Table 2

Distribution of Men and Women Workers in Rural and Urban Sectors in 1961

	Total (in million)		Rural		Urban	
Persons	188.67	(100.00)	162.24	(86.00)	26.43	(14.00)
Men	129.17	(100.00)	106.75	(82.50)	22.42	(17.50)
Women	59.50	(100.00)	55.42	(93.27)	4.01	(6.73)

In most cases the women workers in rural areas are particularly engaged in agriculture and other allied activities. There are several reasons for this: (a) most agricultural operations are simple and do not require any training or skill, (b) womens' employment in agriculture is seasonal in nature and does not require working away from home for a long period, (c) in agricultural works the wages paid to women workers are generally less than the wages paid for men labourers, (d) women probably can be absorbed in works for extra hours much more easily, (e) one of the important reason is that the rural family structure is often such that mothers have less responsibility for childcare, (f) it may be easier to take a child along with them to an agricultural job than to an office or factory. The nature of agricultural occupation is such that the household responsibilities can be easily combined with productive works. In the rural sector most women work as family labourers.[6]

Women work participation rate in rural areas was much higher than that of urban areas in all the states during 1961 and 1971. Only exception was Punjab where urban participation was higher than that of rural in 1971. This was due to the high incidence of women workers found in the service of teaching, caretaker, cleaner, nursing, pharmacist, etc. in urban Punjab.[7] One explanation for the higher work participation of women in rural India could be that women find work easily on the family farms or in the household industries in the rural sector. Even when work has to be done outside family they find it in the close neighbourhood. In the urban sector on the other hand, the scope of women's entrance into the labour force is possibly more restricted, because their participation in work is largely outside the home, and very often a way from the home.

Between rural and urban areas there are always differences in occupational patterns, because education has more influence on women's employment in urban areas than in rural areas. In urban India the occupational structure is more diversified and there is a slow emergence of a new middle class educated working women. Their number has been progressively increasing though the rate of urban women workers is significantly lower than that of rural women.[8] There are also differences in the pattern of services between rural and urban areas. Some major groups in non-household industry command higher rates of women work participation in urban areas. There are a number of occupations and industries in urban areas where women are being employed in increasing number. They are usually teachers, nurses, social education and welfare workers, pediatricians, health service workers, doctors, white-collar workers in manufacturing and other service industries like accountants, book keepers, secretaries and other professionals. The peculiar feature is that there is high percentage of educated women in urban occupations as well as illiterate urban workers are distributed almost equally among the occupational groups such as household and manufacturing industries and sanitary services, etc. In urban area the situation is not much different than that of rural area. Employment pattern of women in both the cases is such that women constitute a very small proportion of all the workers. Out of a total employment the majority of the women workers are engaged in low prestige occupations. A number of city surveys show that the most urban women workers are also uneducated, unskilled and participating in manual occupations. Yet there is gradual but promising increase in modern occupations like teaching, nursing, modern industries, offices, etc.[9] The corresponding level in women work participation in urban India varies from state to state. There was high participation of female workers in urban Punjab in 1971 and was the same in the case of West Bengal also. Whereas in other states such participation was low. This was due to the dominance of women in teaching, building caretaking, nursing and health service occupations both in Punjab and West Bengal.

In a recent study on women's employment pattern based on

1961 census data Mitra, Srimany and Pathak have pointed out to a markedly declining trend in the participation of Indian women in household and non-household industrial activities in both rural and urban areas.[10]

In certain traditional occupations the urban women's work participation was lower than the rural one both in 1961 as well as in 1971. In 1961, rural occupations shared most of the women workers and urban occupation shared only a small portion of the total women workers. During 1971 there was fair participation in traditional occupations in rural sector, but in urban area most of the occupations had low and medium shares. A study of the growth rate of the women work force between 1961 and 1971 showed that in a number of modern urban industries the number of women workers increased six to ten times, as in the manufacture of machinery, electrical appliances, medical and scientific instruments and in trade and banking. At the same time women work force suffered a serious decline in sectors like horticulture, food processing, dairy, jute and textiles. Between rural and urban areas, however, there were differences in the pattern. Educational and scientific services and medical and health services occupied third and fourth places while these represented twentyfifth and tenth positions in rural sector. These findings perhaps imply that education has more effect on women's employment in urban areas than in rural. The higher participation rates of women in some of the traditional activities, however, are almost uniform in both rural and urban areas.[11]

During the last few decades there was an overall decline in the proportion of women workers in the urban sector. In 1951, nearly 11.86 per cent of the total urban women were workers. By 1961 and 1971 this had come down to 11.10 and 10.4 per cent respectively. Although the process of decline was very slow, it represented a clear trend of change in the women work participation.

So far, in the foregoing paragraphs, we have discussed, in general terms, the trend of women work participation. However, this does not differentiate the women work participation in the unorganised and organised sectors of occupations. As our study is concerned with the industrial women workers in tea plantation, it is necessary here to discuss in some detail the women work participation in the organised sector. At the same time women work participation in the unorganised sector is dealt with in brief for a comparative perspective.

WOMEN IN THE UNORGANISED SECTOR

The organised sector is characterized by the absence of protective rules and regulations for workers. As they are generally unregulated no exact information about the terms and conditions of work is available.[12] The workers of the unorganised sector are generally low paid and insecured in employment. They do not have any welfare facilities, but are bound to work more hours.[13] This sector includes agriculture as well as various industries and services. A large number of women are employed in unorganised, small-scale and household industries and occupations.

The 1971 census data showed that there were 31 million women workers of whom 25 million were in agriculture, 2 million in the organised sector, and the remaining 4 million in non-agricultural occupations in the unorganised sector. From this it is seen that 29 million, i.e., 94 per cent of the women workers were engaged in the unorganised sector of which 80.1 per cent were in agriculture and the rest were in non-agricultural occupations. These agricultural women workers constituted 87 per cent of the women work force in rural areas and 17.5 per cent in urban areas.[14]

Women in Agricultural Occupations

The proportion of women workers to total workers is higher in the agricultural sector than in the non-agricultural sector. All the women workers in the agricultural sector are either cultivators or agricultural labourers. The majority of men workers are also in the agricultural sector, but the proportion is higher among the women workers. It is interesting to note that in most of the developed countries the picture is reverse where agriculture is primarily a male activity and the proportion of women workers in the non-agricultural sector is much higher than that of men. In India the proportion of women labour force in agriculture showed an increase from 67 per cent in 1901 to

74 per cent in 1911 and 82 per cent in 1961. Employment outside agriculture recorded a steeper fall from 23 per cent in 1901 to 13.7 per cent in 1961.[15]

All the women workers in the agricultural sector are either cultivators or agricultural labourers. In 1961, 55.7 per cent of such workers were classified as cultivators and the remaining 23.86 per cent as agricultural labourers. In other industrial categories, namely, mining-quarrying-livestock, household industry, manufacturing other than household industry, construction, trade-commerce, transport-storage-communication and other services there were 2 per cent, 7.85 per cent, 1.33 per cent, 0.41 per cent, 1.37 per cent, 0.11 per cent and 7.35 per cent of women workers respectively. Within the agricultural sector, women workers constitute a higher proportion of total workers among agricultural labourers than among cultivators.[16] A sharp decline was visible in the number of women cultivators from 18.3 millions in 1951 to 9.2 million in 1971. This can be attributed to increasing pauperisation leading to the loss of land and inadequate growth of productive employment opportunities on family farms leading to withdrawal of women from active cultivation. There was an increase in the number of women agricultural labourers from 12.6 millions in 1951 to 15.7 millions in 1971.[17]

Women in Non-Agricultural Occupations

In 1961 nearly 20 per cent of the women workers were in non-agricultural occupations in the unorganised sector. This remained constant in the urban sector whereas in the rural sector it declined from 16 to 13 per cent in 1971. There were 46 women workers per 100 men workers in 1961 which came down to 21 in 1971.[18] It seems that women are better represented in the typical household industry or small-scale industry. Very recently Mitra, Pathak and Mukherjee on the basis of 1961 and 1971 census data have shown that the work participation rates among the Indian women is very low, and even if they are in employment they are role gated to very low earning sectors of the economy, demanding strenuous drudge work in low skill and low technology and sectors of low productivity.[19]

Among the non-agricultural occupations, household industry

provides the largest number of employment to the women workers being 39.1 per cent, and lowest number of workers are found to be employed in transport, communication and storage industries.[20] Employment of women in household industries is proportionately higher than that of men. In 1961, the total number of persons at work other than those in cultivation was 57.5 millions of which were 45.4 millions men workers and 12.1 millions women workers. Out of 45.4 millions men workers 7.4 millions (16 per cent) were in household industry, whereas 38 millions were in non-household industry (84 per cent). The share of women in household industry was 4.7 millions (38 per cent), and the remaining 7.4 millions (62 per cent) belonged to non-household industry.[21] The rural-urban distribution of men and women workers during 1961 in household industry are given below (Table 3).

Table 3

Rural-Urban Distribution of Persons in Household Industry, 1961 (in millions)

	Persons in the Household Industry		
	Total Number of Persons	Men	Women
Total	12.1	7.4	4.7
Rural	10.1	6.1	3.9
Urban	2.1	1.3	0.8

The construction workers constitute a significant portion of the unorganised occupational sector. According to the census of 1971 the number of women workers in this occupation was 0.2 million as against 2 million men. Women workers constituted 9.2 per cent of the total workers in this industry and they were employed to perform certain types of labour work. The most important of the unorganised sector where women were employed in large number was the Bidi industries where women constituted about 50 per cent of the total labour force.[22] Chikan industry also absorbed a good number of women workers. Besides there was a good number of women workers who were self employed either as producers or as retailers.

WOMEN IN THE ORGANISED SECTOR

The organised sector includes all public sector establishments and non-agricultural private sector establishments employing ten or more persons. This sector however includes a very small proportion of the women workers in the country. Women have been moving from agriculture to industries and services, and though they now constitute a conspicuous portion of Indian labour force in absolute terms their number is very small. Only 6 per cent women workers in India are found in organised sector.[23]

In the organised sector of economy, the employment of women increased rapidly after 1950. The number of women employed in this sector increased from 1.37 millions in 1962 to 2.14 millions in 1973, i.e., an increase of 56.2 per cent and this increase was faster than the growth rate of total women's employment in India. The women's proportion in the total employment remained practically constant at 11 per cent during 1962-73, whereas women's employment in the organised sector had been steadily growing.

The higher rate of women work participation is found in the household industries and the industries related to textiles, tobacco, etc., whereas the higher rate of women's participation can be found in the non-household industries like water supply and sanitary services, educational and scientific services, medical and health services.[24] Women's employment in the organised sector was 6 per cent in 1971, of which 2.7 per cent was in industry and 3.3 per cent was in services and professions.[25] Although proportion of women workers is low in the total employment but in the organised sector it has been regularly increasing. It increased from 11 per cent in 1971 to 12 per cent in 1977.[26]

Women Workers in Services and Professions

There had been a marginal increase in the women's work participation rate in some white-collar or semi-white-collar occupations, namely, clerks, typists, nurses, pharmacists, stenographers, shop assistants, teachers, cooks and maids as well as in a number of technical and professional sectors.[27] About 7.35 per cent of the women workers were in services like public service, medical and health, education and in other miscellaneous professions. However, employment of women in the government services increased by almost 90.50 per cent during 1951-61.[28]

Marginal increase in the number of women workers in various services and professions was low during 1961-71, and the increase of women workers was mostly in urban occupations except teaching. However, decline was noticed in women work force in the organised and unorganised sectors during 1961-71.

In public sector, the number of women employees had been continuously increasing since 1960's. The number of women workers in administrative, executive and managerial services increased from 10,000 in 1960 to 12,000 in 1966. In the clerical and allied jobs their number went up from 37,000 in 1960 to 79,000 in 1968. Their proportion to total workers in the same year went up from 4.2 to 7.6 per cent. The number of women workers in transport, storage and communication had remained steady. In services, sports and recreation, their number went up from 5,000 to 13,000 during 1960-68, i.e., from 1.1 per cent to 2.4 per cent. The number of women unskilled office workers decreased from 25,000 to 16,000

In the private sector the number showed a steady increase in clerical and allied jobs, sports and recreation work and school teaching. The decline was marked among administrative, executive and managerial workers from 5,000 to 1,000 and professional, technical and related workers from 55,000 to 31,000 during 1963-70.[29] There were a number of occupations and industries where number of women workers had been gradually increasing. Such occupations, where reservations for females were often maintained, were the jobs of teachers, nurses, community health workers, pediatricians, nutritionists, social education and welfare workers, blue and white-collar workers in manufacturing, construction, trade and commerce, transport and service industries, etc.

It is difficult to give a correct statistical profile of women in services and professions. From the available data two trends are clearly visible: (i) there is a concentration of women in the teaching and medicine and (ii) certain low prestigious jobs in the clerical services are suited to women.[30]

Women in the Organised Industry

In India women have always been employed in factories, plantations and mines. During the last few decades there had been a continuous decline in the number of working women in the organised industries (Table 4). The total employment of men and women in various industries during 1961 was 34,97,000 which gradually increased up to 41,60,000 in 1970. But the average employment of women gradually decreased during this period. In 1961 there were 3,72,334 women workers and in 1970 their number decreased to 3,69,198.[31]

In the organised industries a constant decline in the percentage of women to the total workers has been recorded during the last several decades (Table 4). A marked decline in textile, cotton and jute industries has been attributed to technological changes in the manufacturing processes in which women are considered unsuitable. However, a decline in the daily average employment of women in manufacturing industries as well as in some other industries which can be safely called urban in nature confirms that a substantial decline is taking place in the urban sector. The decline in the factory employment is accompanied by an increase in the service group such as public service, medical and education and the large chunk of miscellaneous categories.[32]

The following table gives us information about the number of women employed in factories and their percentage to the total number of employees for the years 1929, 1934, 1939, 1946, 1951, 1955 and from 1960 to 1970.[33]

It is seen from the table that though the number of women employees increased, the percentage went down from 14.85 per cent in 1934 to 9.00 per cent in 1970. It is also interesting that the number which went up to 4.09 lakhs in 1964 came down to 3.69 lakhs in 1970.

Table 4

Average Daily Employment of Women in Factories

Year	Number of Women Employees ('000)	Percentage of Women to Total Employees
1934	220.86	14.85
1939	243.52	13.90
1946	272.00	11.75
1951	290.00	11.43
1955	295.10	10.96
1960	367.30	10.90
1961	372.30	10.64
1962	394.10	10.80
1963	400.40	10.37
1964	409.10	10.16
1965	394.50	9.57
1966	364.70	8.96
1967	394.00	9.50
1968	346.00	9.00
1969	382.00	9.00
1970	369.00	9.00

Though total employment in factories has been increasing steadily, women's employment in the organised sector of industry has been decreasing since 1961 (Tables 5,6,7). While the number of total employees has increased, the number of women employees has declined. Employment of women in major factory industries in 1961 was 4,20,090 and in 1970 it came down to 2,32,893. The number of women workers in 1961 in industries allied to agriculture was 49,480 and in food industries it was 1,06,250, in tobacco industries it was 84,165, in textiles it was 67,979 and in miscellaneous industries it was 77,692. In the year 1970 these numbers came down to 43,483 in industries allied to agriculture, 1,15,845 in food industries, 64,769 in tobacco industries and 10,855 in miscellaneous industries. Only in case of industries related to chemical and chemical products the number of women increased from 14,548 to 20,689 and in non-metallic mineral industries their employment increased from 22,976 to 26,213 (Table 5). In mines their number declined from 109,000 to 75,000 during 1951 and 1971, whereas the total employment increased from 549,000 to 630,000. The number of women workers in mines declined from 21.1 per cent to 11.9 per cent, in coal mines this decline was more, i.e., from 55,000 to 2,000. The ban on employment of women in underground mining from 1951 must have been partly responsible for the decline of women work participation in mines.[35] From 1952-1969 there was a decline of women in the mines (Table 6 and 7).

Table 5

Women Employed in Major Factory Industries

		1961	1970
1.	Process Allied to Agriculture	49,480	43,483
2.	Food (Except Beverage)	1,06,250	1,15,845
3.	Tobacco	84,165	64,769
4.	Textiles	67,979	51,039
5.	Chemicals and Chemical Products	14,548	20,689
6.	Non-metallic Mineral Products (except Petroleum and Coal Products	22,976	26,213
7.	Miscellaneous Industries	77,692	10,855
		4,20,090	2,32,893

Table 6

Decline of Women Workers in·Mines (in percentage)

Mines	Year	
	1952	1962
Coal Mines	14.8	8.9
Iron-ore Mines	35.6	26.7
Mica Mines	21.1	8.4
Manganese Mines	42.4	39.9

Table 7

Employment of Women in Mines
(in thousands)

Year	No. of Women (in thousands)
1961	106.3
1966	100.3
1967	90.9
1968	84.3
1969	78.0

Besides mines, women's employment declined considerably in textile and jute industries. The process of heavy mechanisation which has taken place in such industries have deprived the women workers from employment. The women workers have been alienated due to lack of skill in handling modern machines.[37] Industries with capital intensive technology displace women rather than men. Process of displacement is justified on the ground that as women are illiterate they are unwilling to learn new processes and skills. In the labour intensive industries like plantations there has been no displacement of women.[38]

Women Workers in Plantation

In most Asian plantations with a family employment policy, women and children work together with the men workers. In Ceylon and Vietnam women account for over 50 per cent of the labour force in plantations. In Malay and India the share is over 40 per cent and in Pakistan and Philippines it is around 35 per cent.[39]

The special feature of Indian plantation industry is that it not only employs the men members but also women and children above the age of 12 years of the families, and women have an important role to play. The reasons for this are: (a) the plantation work is only a special kind of agricultural work and is therefore, familiar to Indian women, the vast majority of whom live in rural areas, (b) facilities have been given to make workers to settle on, or in the vicinity of the plantations and to take their wives and families with them and (c) under the old system, labour contract was based on the principle of utilising every able bodied persons of the family of labour and fixing the wage rates accordingly; many women had to seek employment in order to balance the family budget; although the contract system has been abolished, the wage system and the need for supplementary earnings still remain.[40]

Plantation is the only non-household industry in the organised sector where women's employment has not declined. In tea plantation the number of women workers increased from 250,000 to 270,000 between 1954 and 1962, i.e., an increase from 46.1 per cent to 49.2 per cent. A marginal increase in the number of women workers was also noticed in coffee and rubber plantations.[41] It is interesting to note that the increase in the number of workers in the labour force recorded in tea plantation is due to the increase in the number of women as well as men workers. But the increase of women's employment is more than that of men (Table 8.)

In 1961, the women workers constituted 44 per cent of the total labour force in tea plantation. They constituted 45.3 per cent of the total labour force in coffee plantation and there were 21.4 per cent of women workers in the total labour force in rubber plantation. But in 1970 these figures changed to 47 per cent for tea, 44 per cent for coffee and 35 per cent for rubber plantations. From this it is clearly seen that during the period from 1961 to 1970 the number of women workers in tea and rubber plantations increased but in coffee plantations their number decreased. Therefore in tea plantation there had been 3 per cent rise in the number of women workers from 1960 to 1970.[42] It is also seen that the women work participation is generally high in all types of plantations, the highest being in the tea plantation. These figures are also higher than the percentage of women employed in any other industry or mines (Table 4 and 6). In comparison to other industrial sectors tea industry experiences regular increase of women labourers since its establishment. Several factors work behind it. Recruitment of the tea labourers is made mainly from among the Adivasis of neighbouring states. As the tea industry is agro-based the Adivasi women do not find much difficulty to adjust themselves in the new working environment. On the other hand, as tea industry requires limited mechanisation there is a constant rise in the number of women workers. The limited mechanisation in tea industry always suits to the physical strength of women labourers. Plantation industry generally prefers to recruit family members of the workers so that it helps to develop the occupations as a family unit. This has resulted in the regular recruitment of the women workers in this industry. The other important reason, however, is the traditionally accepted lower wage rate for women workers in the tea industry.

In 1961, the plantation work was a major women employing occupation in Assam, West Bengal and Tamil Nadu. In Assam, more than 95 per cent of the women workers in the organised sector were plantation labourers. West Bengal provided the largest chunk of non-agricultural women workers being 19 per cent. Almost 80 per cent of these women were labourers in tea plantations.[43] In Assam their number rose to 70 per cent in 1971 achieving the status of topmost women employing non-agricultural occupation of whom most were labourers almost entirely in tea industry. In Tamil Nadu and West Bengal women work participation rate in non-agricultural occupations had also increased.

Table 8

Estimated Number of Labourers Employed in Tea Plantation in India in 1973, 1977 and 1980

	Average Daily Number of Labourers Employed					
	1973		1977		1980	
	Men	Women	Men	Women	Men	Women
West Bengal	85,032	92,901	87,289	96,255	97,374	100,388
North India	275,214	277,354	277,358	278,531	303,080	296,098
South India	55,461	81,924	68,080	80,475	69,205	88,543
All India	330,775	359,278	345,438	359,006	372,285	384,641

From the above table (Table 8) it is revealed that although there was a slight decline in the number of the plantation women workers from 359,278 to 359,006 in 1977 at the all India level, in case of West Bengal their number had increased, i.e., from 92,901 in 1973 to 96,255 in 1977. A similar trend was also noticed in North India. But in South India number of women workers in tea plantations declined during the same period. On the other hand, in all these regions as well as at the all India level number of men workers in tea plantations increased steadily. In 1980 there was steady rise of women workers in plantation being 384,641 at the all India level. In the same year in West Bengal the number of women workers in plantation increased upto 100,388.[44] The increase in the number of plantation women workers as well as men workers in West Bengal had been due to some reasons. This was due to an extensive labour movement among the tea garden workers in West Bengal in 1969 leading to a total strike for sixteen days and the major demand was for increasing labour force in tea gardens. The trade unions demanded that a land-labour ratio of 1.5 workers per acre of land should be maintained. However the compromise was made on 1.1.[45] The result of which was the new recruitment followed by slight increase in both the men and women labour force in West Bengal since 1973 onwards.

From the above discussion it is revealed that the great majority of women workers in India are engaged either in agriculture and traditional rural industries or in service occupations. Though the majority of workers in the agricultural sector in rural areas are men but the proportion of women workers is also very high. One of the plausible explanation for such high rate of women work participation in rural area could be that the rural women find themselves easily adjusted on the family farms or in the household industries in rural sector. On the other hand, in the urban sector the scope for women workers is much more restricted as in most cases the working places are situated long away from their home.

In diversified urban occupations there is a slow emergence of a new middle class educated women. Their number is gradually increasing though the work participation rate of urban women is significantly lower than the rural women. In urban area educated women are employed in large number in occupations like teaching, nursing, social welfare and education, medical practice, accountancy, book-keeping, secretaries, etc. Illiterate urban women are equally distributed in occupations like household and manufacturing industries and sanitary services, etc. In urban Punjab the women work participation is high in comparison to other states. It is also seen that there is a declining tendency of participation of women in household and non-household industrial activities and so also in horticulture, food processing industry, dairy, jute and textiles. During the last few decades there has been a declining tendency of women employment in the urban sector.

The proportion of women workers in the agricultural occupations of the unorganised sector is always higher than the non-agricultural occupations. The women's employment in non-agricultural sector recorded a steep fall in between 1901 and 1971. In agricultural sector a sharp decline of women cultivators was visible in between 1951 and 1971 which came down from 18.3 million to 9.2 millions. This may be due to loss of land, inadequate growth of productive employment opportunities in family farms. In non-agricultural occupations urban women workers remained constant whereas the rural workers work-participation slightly declined. Women always better represented in typical household or small-scale industry. In India the general work participation rate of women workers was low.

Women construction workers constitute a significant portion of the labour force and they are employed in large number in Bidi industries in the unorganised sector. Women constitute nearly 50 per cent of the labour force in Bidi industries. In the unorganised sector there is also a good number of women employed as producers or retailers.

In the organised sector in general, women work participation is appreciably lower than that in unorganised sector. The employment of women in this sector increased rapidly after 1950 at a rate faster than the growth rate of total women work force though in proportion to men their employment declined during this period (Table 4).

Women workers are mostly employed in tea, coffee, rubber and coconut plantations, tobacco curing and match industry, coir, making, carpet weaving and food processing industry. They are also employed in certain occupations like sanitary services, educational and scientific services, medical and health services, etc. There has been a marginal increase of women workers in occupations like clerks, typists, nurses, pharmacists, stenographers, teachers, shop assistants, cooks and maids, etc. In services, sports and recreation their number is also increasing. At the same time the number of women unskilled office workers is decreasing.

There has been a marked and continuous decline in the number of working women in organised industry though total employment in factories has been increasing. There is a marked decline in the number of women workers in coal mine. The ban on employment of women in underground mining is partly responsible for this. Besides mines, there is decline of women's employment in major textile and jute industries which is due to heavy mechanisation of such industries. These capital intensive industries displace women rather than men whereas in labour intensive industries like plantations there has been no displacement of women workers. The whole family of the workers get their livelihood from this industry. In tea plantation there is a marked increase in the number of women workers and a marginal increase in coffee and rubber plantations. Tea industry requires limited mechanisation and there is a constant rise of women's employment in tea industries. Specially tea plantation of Assam and West Bengal and coffee plantation of Tamil Nadu are the major women employing industry in the organised sector. In between the period 1973 and 1977 and 1980 the number of women workers in tea plantations of West Bengal increased from 92,301 to 96,255 and to 100, 388 respectively. The trend was same in North India, but in South India it was declining. The growing number of women workers in tea plantation in West Bengal draw our attention in the study of women industrial workers in tea plantation.

In summing up the whole discussion it seems that barring a small number of white-collar jobs held almost exclusively by middle-class working women, the vast majority of working women are employed in labour intensive jobs whether they are in factories or plantation or in agriculture. The demand for women workers remains constant or increases depending upon the state of development of these sectors. But if some degree of mechanisation sets in any industry it is the women who become the first victims of unemployment probably because they are employed as unskilled labourers.

References

1. Sinha, J.N., "The Indian Working Force: Its Growth and Changing Composition" in *Census of India, 1961*, Vol. I., Monograph No.11. Office of the Registrar General, India, Ministry of Home Affairs, New Delhi, 1971, pp. 113-26.
2. Mitra, A., L.P. Pathak and S. Mukherjee, *The Status of Women — Shifts in Occupational Participation 1961-71,* Abhinav Publications, New Delhi, 1980, p. 46.
3. Nath, K., "Women in the Working Force in India" in *Economic and Political Weekly,* Vol. III, No. 31, August 3, 1968., p. 1205.
4. D'Souza, V.S., "Family Status and Female Work Participation" in A. D'Souza (ed.), *Women in Contemporary India and South Asia,* Manohar, New Delhi, 1980, pp. 125-126.
5. Nath, K., op.cit., p.1206.
6. Gulati, L., "Female Work Participation" in *Economic and Political Weekly,* Vol. X, no.1 and 2, January 11, 1975, p.36.
7. Mitra, A., L.P. Pathak and S. Mukherjee., op.cit. p. 67.
8. Nath, K., "Urban Women Workers" in *Economic Weekly*, Vol. XVIII, N. 37, September 11, 1965.

9. Gadgil, D.R., *Poona: A Socio-Economic Survey,* Gokhale Institute of Politics and Economics, Poona, 1945. Sen, S.N., *The city of Calcutta — A Socio-Economic Survey,* 1954-55 to 1957-58, Calcutta, Book Land, 1960, p. 6.
10. Mitra, A., A. Srimany and L.P. Pathak, *Status of Women: Household and Non-household Economic Activity,* Allied Publishers, ICSSR, Programme of Women's Studies, New Delhi, 1979, pp. 1-9.
11. Mitra, A., L.P. Pathak and S. Mukherjee, op. cit., p. 50.
12. For details see Karnik, V.B., *Indian Labour-Problems and Prospects,* Minerva Associates (Publications) Pvt. Ltd., Calcutta, 1974, p. 73.
13. ICSSR, *Status of Women in India,* Allied Publishers Pvt. Ltd. 1975, p. 68.
14. *Ibid.,* pp. 63-65.
15. Sinha, J.N. op. cit., pp. 113-126.
16. Nath, K., op. cit., August 3, 1968, p. 1207
17. ICSSR., op. cit., p. 65.
18. Mitra, A., L.P. Pathak and S. Mukherjee, op. cit., 1980, p.63.
19. *Ibid.,* p. 48.
20. Nath, K., op. cit., p. 1207.
21. Mitra, A., A.K. Srimany and L.P. Pathak, op. cit., p. 5.
22. Karnik, V.B., op. cit., p. 73.
23. ICSSR, op. cit., p. 63.
24. Mitra, A.,op. cit., p. 59.
25. ICSSR, op. cit., p. 63.
26. Mitra, A., L.P. Pathak and S. Mukherjee, op. cit., p. 50.
27. Mitra, A., L.P. Pathak and S. Mukherjee, ibid., p. 77.
28. Srivastava, V., *Employment of Educated Married Women in India,* National Publishing House, New Delhi, 1978, p. 14.
29. ICSSR, op. cit., pp. 75-76.
30. ICSSR, ibid., p. 76.
31. *Indian Labour Statistics,* 1972, p. 37.
32. Srivastava, V., op. cit., pp. 14, 16.
33. Ibid., p. 16.
    Karnik, V.B., op. cit., pp. 70-71.
34. *Indian Labour Statistics,* op. cit., p. 36.
35. Mitra, A., 1979, op. cit., p. 45.
36. *Indian Labour Statistics,* 1971.
37. Karnik, V.B. op. cit., p. 71.

38. ICSSR, op. cit., p. 74.
39. Boserup, E., *Woman's Role in Economic Development,* George Allen & Unwin, London, 1970, p. 76.
40. ILO (International Labour Organization), *Industrial Labour in India,* Series A, Industrial Relations, No. 41, Geneva, 1938, pp. 35-36.
41. ICSSR, op. cit., p. 72.
42. *Ibid.*, p. 165.
43. Mitra, A., L.P. Pathak and S. Mukherjee, op. cit., 1980, p. 106.
44. *Tea Statistics,* Tea Board of India, 1976, pp. 100-103; 1978-79, pp. 112-115, 1981-82, p. 125.
45. Bhowmik, S., *Class Formation in the Plantation System,* Peoples Publishing House, New Delhi, 1981, p. 8.

Chapter 3

Background of the Tea Plantation

The present chapter, firstly, deals with the growth of plantation industry in West Bengal, and secondly, it describes the basic features of a tea plantation industry of Darjeeling district along with its population, hierarchical system, characteristics of the men and women workers and their ethnic background, religion, literacy and migration.

GROWTH OF THE PLANTATION IN WEST BENGAL

The history of tea industry in India goes back to 1820 when tea plant was discovered growing wild in Assam. In 1835, the first tea plantation was started in Assam by the British Government.[1] Gradually West Bengal was found suitable for tea cultivation and experimentally tea plantations were established. The tea producing area in West Bengal are Darjeeling, Dooars and Terai regions. In Darjeeling district the Kurseong and Darjeeling Tea Company opened the first tea garden known as Alubari in 1856 and in Jalpaiguri district Gazelduba garden was started in Dooars in 1874. In the Terai region of Darjeeling district the first tea garden was started in Champta near Khaprail in 1862 and by 1866 many other plantations were opened in this region.[2] In this year there were 39 tea plantations occupying 10,000 acres of land of the district. There was a regular increase in the number of plantations.

In 1895 there came up 186 plantations with 48,692 acres of land. Since 1896 there had been a continuous decrease in the number of plantations and in 1935 it came down to 148 plantations which occupied 59,356 acres of land. Again there was a fall in the number and in 1940 their number was recorded as 142 occupying 63,059 acres of land. The area occupied by the plantations increased upto 63,227 acres in 1943.[3] Therefore it is revealed that while the number of tea gardens had been decreased the acreage under tea had increased between 1896 and 1943. Such decrease in the number of tea gardens was perhaps due to the fact that some small gardens merged with one another or with a bigger one. However, most of the gardens had increased the acreage under tea cultivation.

The development of tea plantations required two basic requisites: a large area for cultivation and a large labour force. The tea regions of West Bengal were either sparsely populated or the local people rarely worked on plantation because of the low wages offered by the planters. In 1931 the basic wage rates in Darjeeling hills were 5 annas for men, 4 annas for women and 3 annas for children and in Terai plantations it was 4 annas for men, 3 annas for women and $1\frac{1}{2}$ annas for children.[4] It was 4 annas for men, 3 annas for women and 3 annas for children in Dooars.[5] Such basic wages were prevalent for a long time. It was reported that the local agricultural abourers in adjoining villages earned more without difficulty. Perhaps these people would not have liked to give up their ndependent holdings to work on tea garden.[6] Since local abourers were not willing to work on plantations, the planters ad to look elsewhere for the supply of cheap and hardworking abourers.

The plantation all over the world is survived on imported abourers who are comparatively cheaper than the local labourers. n tea plantation, planters had to depend on indentured labourers om outside. Thus the immigrant labourers become an inseparable art of the plantation system. Plantation is by and large associated ith a resident labour force which is of alien origin.

Rapid growth of tea plantations within a very short period xperienced a labour crisis in this region. In Darjeeling district ere were not only tea plantations but also a number of hincona plantations on the hills. Chincona plantations further dded to the labour crisis in the region. This demand was then lfilled by a large scale immigration into the tea districts. The immigrants were mainly Adivasis (tribals) from Chotanagpur region of Bihar, Raigarh of Madhya Pradesh and from several feudatory states of Orissa. In the hill regions the majority were Nepali immigrants. In the Terai region the population was mixed with a low proportion of Nepalis and a high proportion of immigrated Adivasi people. The local people like Meches, Rajbansis, etc. rarely worked in tea plantations. Low wages and hazardous conditions of work provided strong disincentives for the local population. Therefore the industry had to look elsewhere for supply of labour.

It was not possible to state the exact number of men and women workers separately during the different stages of migration of tea labourers in Darjeeling and Jalpaiguri districts as no such systematic data were available. However, Dash noted that in tea industry of Darjeeling district there were 8,000 members in 1870, 44,279 were employed in 1921 and 61,540 were in 1940.[7]

Like Dooars almost entire labour force in the tea plantations in Terai consisted of immigrants and their descendents. The plantation workers in Terai were never placed under any contract. In this sense they were 'free' labourers as found in Dooars. But in Assam they were like bondage labourers. Some garden managers frequently tried to entice workers from other gardens to avoid the recruiting costs. In order to prevent such enticement of labourers some code was formed by the Terai Planters Association.

In Darjeeling district there were 56 gardens in 1870 out of which 44 were in the hills and 12 in the Terai region. The total labourers were 8,347 of whom 4,484 were men, 2,935 were women and 928 were children. During the four years following 1870, the tea industry in Darjeeling continued to develop and by 1874 the number of plantations had increased from 56 to 113. The cultivated area rose from 11,046 acres to 18,888 acres and the labourers employed rose from 8,347 to 19,424. During that period the increase of labourers was very satisfactory. It was seen that within the years between 1866 and 1874 the number of gardens under tea plantations had almost exactly trebled, and the area under tea cultivation had increased by 82 per cent.[8] The problem of shortage of labour existed for nearly eighty years since the foundation of tea industry in the Darjeeling district in 1866. The tea industry was rapidly expanding as the number of tea gardens increased (Table 9).[9]

Table 9

Tea Industry in the Darjeeling District, 1866-1874

Year	Number of Gardens	Area in Acres	No. of Labourers Employed
1866	39	10,392	Not Known
1867	40	9,214	
1868	44	10,067	6,859
1869	55	10,769	7,445
1870	56	11,046	8,347
1871	—	—	—
1872	74	14,503	12,361
1873	87	15,695	14,019
1874	113	18,888	19,424

A striking feature of the labour force in plantation in the country in 1944, about which the Labour Investigation Committee had made a specific mention, was the employment of women and children in large numbers in all the centres. In Assam and Bengal the labour force comprised an almost equal number of men and women, and in South India women outnumbered men workers. It was significant to note that women workers outnumbered men in all the regions of the country. The main reasons were as follows. The recruitment of workers was on a family basis rather than on an individual basis. The work in plantations was akin to that of agriculture, and women workers hailing from rural areas had no difficulty in picking up the works. Migration of workers along with their families placed almost an obligation on management to provide work to members of worker's family as well. For this reason all the previous data available on plantation were based on workers in general. Women workers were never treated as a distinct group of workers in the light of historical evidences. Therefore, very little data were available on the historical background leading to the employment of women in tea industry of Terai though they were asset to this industry.

However, the number of women workers was found to be constant or slightly increased. It was found that their number was higher in comparison to the men workers. In 1939, of the working population in the tea plantation in Darjeeling district, 39 per cent were men, 43 per cent were women and 18 per cent were children. Figure for 1943 showed that men made up 34 per cent, women 49 per cent and children 17 per cent.[10] Gradually the number of workers increased and the planters overcame the crisis of labour shortage. Since migration was family-based, and since very few people returned to their places of origin, the children of the workers soon became the job-seekers. However, tea industry in Darjeeling district was expanding till 1950's. After 1950's the industry stopped migration as there were surplus labourers. In 1952 the Plantation Labour Act was passed to protect the men and women workers in plantation. Now the feudalistic relations between planters and the workers changed to a relationship of employers and employees. The plantation workers were given some legal protection and there was scope to form their own association. Since the Plantation Labour Act was effective for permanent workers, the planters wanted to reduce the number of permanent workers as this would decrease the overhead costs. Consequently, there was a reduction in the labour force since the passing of the Plantation Labour Act, 1951. However, no exact data were available for particularly the women plantation workers although the Tea Board of India maintained systematic data on plantation labourers of West Bengal as well as of different states of the country. Only after 1960 district-wise data on men, women and children workers were available. Table 10 shows a clear trend of decreasing labour force in West Bengal upto the year 1980.

In 1970 there was an increase in the number of labour employed in tea plantations. This was due to the extensive labour movement in West Bengal in 1969. A major demand in that strike was that the number of labour force of the tea gardens should be increased. The trade unions demanded for a land-labour ratio of 1:1.5 for every acre of land. Lastly there was a compromise at 1:1.1. In 1977 in West Bengal the number of tea estate was 298 and the area under tea cultivation

Table 10

Declining Plantation Labour Force in West Bengal and India, 1950-1980

Year	West Bengal	India
1950	329,034	1,033,090
1951	265,064	1,017,989
1952	322,679	1,054,295
1953	266,753	969,610
1954	283,593	993,594
1955	273,163	989,656
1956	268,671	1,004,683
1957	261,384	997,491
1958	251,145	980,238
1959	236,674	919,405
1960	N.A.	N.A.
1961	N.A.	N.A.
1962	189,968	816,262
1963	196,404	847,372
1964	195,046	818,783
1965	191,702	806,152
1966	191,593	804,135
1967	187,612	775,183
1968	189,745	755,729
1969	187,840	747,835
1970	200,280	759,646
1971	198,074	766,593
1972	194,901	761,919
1973	196,159	766,036
1974	199,793	771,717
1975	200,130	774,897
1976	200,049	776,162
1977	205,466	778,673
1978	223,731	882,140
1979	227,437	924,239
1980	228,705	912,522

Source: *Tea Statistics*, Tea Board of India, Calcutta, 1957, p. 49; 1959, p. 53; 1968-69, p. 89; 1969-70, p. 92; 1977-78, pp. 102-103; 1978-79, pp. 106-109; 1981-82, p. 125.

was 89,253 hectares and average number of labourers were 205,466. The average labour per hectare was 2.3 (Table 11).

Recent statistics of tea plantation also showed that women workers still outnumbered men workers at the all India level. In 1977 men workers were 345,438 and women workers were 359,006 in tea plantation in India. In this year West Bengal, Tripura, Bihar, Tamil Nadu, Karnataka and Kerala showed a similar trend in employment pattern in tea plantations. In 1977 number of women workers in tea plantations of West Bengal was 96,255 (Table 12). In West Bengal in this year number of plantation women workers was higher in the Darjeeling and Terai regions while in Dooars, West Dinajpur and Cooch Bihar men workers were more than the women workers (Table 13).

During the year 1977 field labourers employed in Terai plantations were 7,099 men, 8,690 women, 427 adolescent and 1,490 children. Among the factory labourers there were 1,600 men, 288 women and 14 children.[11] From this it was revealed that the number of women workers in tea plantation was higher than that of men workers and in case of field labourers and it was higher than factory labourers.

Table 11

Number of Tea Plantation, Area and Labourers Employed in Different States of India in 1977

State	Number of Tea Estates	Area in hectare	Estimated Average Daily Number of Labourers	Labour per hectare
Assam	756	190,621	410,520	2.15
West Bengal	298	89,253	205,466	2.30
Tripura	56	5,600	8,380	1.50
Bihar	3	459	223	0.49
Uttar Pradesh	31	1,799	1,259	0.70
Himachal Pradesh	1385	4,183	8,139	1.95
Tamil Nadu	6561	36,333	80,499	2.22
Karnataka	15	1,834	3,855	2.10
Kerala	4124	36,194	70,332	1.94
All India	13,229	366,276	788,673	2.15

Source: *Tea Statistics 1978-79*, Tea Board of India, Calcutta, pp. 116-117.

Table 12

State-wise and Category-wise Estimated Average Daily Number of Labour Employed in Tea Industry During the Year 1977

State	Estimated Average Daily Number of Labour Employed				
	Male	Female	Adolescent	Children	Total
Assam	182,836	173,241	14,513	39,930	410,520
West Bengal	87,289	96,255	8,003	13,919	205,466
Tripura	3,405	4,104	97	774	8,380
Bihar	73	150	—	—	223
Uttar Pradesh	374	854	—	31	1,259
Himachal Pradesh	3,381	3,927	323	508	8,139
Tamil Nadu	36,000	41,460	2,904	135	80,499
Karnataka	1,779	1,823	192	61	3,855
Kerala	30,301	37,192	2,094	945	70,332
All India	345,438	359,006	28,126	56,103	788,673

Source: *Tea Statistics 1978-79*, Tea Board of India, Calcutta, pp. 112, 115.

Table 13

District-wise and Category-wise Estimated Average Daily Number of Labour Employed in Tea Industry of West Bengal During the Year 1977

Region	Estimated Average Daily Number of Labour Employed				
	Male	Female	Adolescent	Children	Total
Darjeeling	15,612	27,550	1,167	1,983	46,312
Terai	8,699	8,978	427	1,504	19,608
Dooars	62,432	59,330	6,407	10,432	138,601
West Dinajpur	352	244	—	—	596
Cooch Bihar	194	153	2	—	349
Total	87,289	96,255	8,003	13,919	205,466

Source: *Tea Statistics 1978-79*, Tea Board of India, Calcutta, p. 112.

CHANDMONI TEA ESTATE

The plantation under study known as Chandmoni Tea Estate was established in 1922. It is situated in the Terai area just at the fringe of the Siliguri town of Darjeeling district and by the side of the National Highway No. 31 on which buses ply frequently. Due to its location near the urban centre Adivasi workers of the plantation have been considerably influenced by the urban way of life.

Population

The area under tea cultivation in Chandmoni is about 450.94 acres, but the local area of the plantation is slightly more. The total number of households is 293 of which 276 belong to the workers having a population of 1252 and 17 to the non-managerial and managerial staff having a population of 75. "The number of men and women workers engaged permanently in the plantation is 515. Out of 276 labour households 246 (89.13 per cent) belong to Adivasi communities having a population of 1,098 (87.70 per cent) and 30 (10.87 per cent) belong to the non-tribal communities having a population of 154 (12.30 per cent, Tables 14, 15 and 16).

Population of the plantation consists of multi-ethnic communities (Table 14). The workers belong to various Adivasi communities of Bihar, Madhya Pradesh and Orissa origin. Besides, there are a few Biharis, Bengalis and Nepalis. Among the Adivasis there are 90 (36.58 per cent) households of Oraons, 53 (21.54 per cent) of Mundas, 8 (3.25 per cent) of Kherias, 17 (6.91 per cent) of Baraiks, 19 (9.72 per cent) of Ghasis, 10 (4.06 per cent) of Malpaharis, 7 (2.84 per cent) of Mahalis, 6 (2.44 per cent) each of Koras and Lohars, 5 (2.03 per cent) each of Saosis and Goswamis, 4 (1.63 per cent) each of Bhoktas, Turis and Goalas, 2(0.81 per cent) each of Mehers and Bairagis and 1 (0.40 per cent) each of Gonds, Bhuiyans, Routias and Ores. Among the non-Adivasis there are 1 (3.33 per cent) Bengali, 9 (30.00 per cent) Behari and 20 (66.66 per cent) Nepali households (Tables 14, 15, 16).

Table 14

Distribution of Adivasi Workers

Ethnic Group	Number of Households	%	Population				
			Male	Female	Children	Total	%
Oraon	90	36.58	132	133	163	428	38.97
Munda	53	21.54	85	72	89	246	22.40
Kheria	8	3.25	15	12	9	36	3.27
Meher	2	0.81	4	3	3	10	0.91
Gond	1	0.40	2	1	1	4	0.36
Baraik	17	6.91	29	21	18	68	6.19
Goswami	5	2.03	6	6	5	17	1.54
Saosi	5	2.03	6	6	5	17	1.54
Bairagi	2	0.81	3	3	4	10	0.91
Goala	4	1.63	5	2	1	8	0.72
Malpahari	10	4.06	11	15	11	37	3.36
Mahali	7	2.84	10	10	12	32	2.91
Bhokta	4	1.63	5	8	4	17	1.54
Ghasi	19	7.72	32	23	31	86	7.83
Korowa	6	2.44	8	8	11	27	2.45
Routia	1	0.40	1	2	2	5	0.45
Bhuiyan	1	0.40	1	—	—	1	0.09
Lohar	6	2.44	10	10	12	32	2.91
Turi	4	1.63	6	3	5	14	1.27
Ore	1	0.40	2	1	—	3	0.27
Total	246	100.00	373	339	386	1098	100.00

Table 15

Distribution of Caste Workers

Caste Group	Number of Households	%	Population				
			Male	Female	Children	Total	%
Bengali							
Brahmin	1	3.33	1	—	—	1	0.64
Behari							
Khusbaha	1	3.33	1	—	—	1	0.64
Muchi	1	3.33	4	2	—	6	3.89
Hazam	1	33.3	2	1	1	4	2.59
Kurmi	1	3.33	3	3	_	6	3.89

Routh	1	3.33	1	2	5	8	5.19
Brahmin	4	13.33	9	3	—	12	7.79
Nepali							
Kami	4	13.33	8	7	14	29	18.83
Thami	2	6.66	2	6	—	8	5.10
Rai	8	10.00	6	5	2	13	8.44
Prodhan	1	3.33	3	4	—	7	4.54
Chhettri	5	16.66	12	8	15	35	22.72
Brahmin	5	16.66	6	8	10	24	15.58
Total	30	(100.00)	58	49	47	154	(100.00)

Table 16

Total Labour Population (Adivasi and Caste)

Social Group	Number of Households	%	Population				
			Male	Female	Children	Total	%
Adivasi	246	89.13	373	339	386	1,098	87.70
Caste	30	10.87	58	49	47	154	12.30
Total	276	(100.00)	431	388	433	1252	(100.00)

Residence

The plantation provides ten residential areas for the workers known as "labour lines" where housing facilities are available for the workers' families. Only in the two residential areas there are brick houses and in the rest of the residential areas there are mud houses. At the centre of the plantation there is the residential area having brick building for the managerial and other office staff of the plantation. It is noticed that similar to other industrial communities the plantation has a heterogeneous population who live interspersed in the labour lines. Therefore, there is no residential segregation according to tribal and caste communities in the plantation. Only the Bihari caste groups are segregated in the Gudam Line situated very near to the manager's bunglow. Such multi-ethnic residential pattern is non-traditional.

The distribution of houses in the ten residential blocks, i.e., the 'labour lines' is not equal. The highest concentration of houses is found in the Bara Line which has 110 households followed by Itabhatta Line 40, Champta Line 34, Dibroo Line 30, Hospital Line 20, Philip Line 19, Matigara Line 9, Gudam Line 7, Tetu Line 5 and Dhansera Line 2 households. However there is some concentration of ethnic groups in these residential lines. In Bara Line majority are Oraons. Bhoktas are concentrated in Matigara Line, Biharis are in Gudam Line, Nepalis are in Barà Line and Habhatta Line.

Households

The data on the households of the plantation reveal the complexity of identifying their types as well as their composition. It is found that some individuals who live in a family in certain cases are unrelated members. However, without going into details of the definition and composition of the two types of families, namely, nuclear and joint, which are beyond the scope of the present study, it is better to discuss the distribution of the households of the plantation into these two types of family. The average size of the workers' households is 4.53 members and the size of the family varies from 1 to 10 members. On an average there are 2.43 workers per family.

In the plantation there are 276 workers' households of which 60 (21.74 per cent) are of joint type and 208 (75.36 per cent) are of nuclear type and 8 (2.90 per cent) are unclassified. Among the Malpharis, Baraiks, Oraons, Ghasis, Nepalis, Mundas, etc. nuclear families are predominantly found. All the households of the Malpaharis are nuclear. About 82.35 per cent, 80.00 per cent, 74.44 per cent, 73.62 per cent, and 67.92 per cent of the households of the Baraiks, Nepalis, Oraons, Ghasis, and Mundas respectively are nuclear (Table 17).

Table 17

Ethnic Groups and Household Types

Ethnic Group	Number of Households	Types of Households		
		Joint	Nuclear	Unclassified
Adivasi				
Oraon	90	22	67	1
Munda	53	14	36	3
Kheria	8	2	6	—

Meher	2	1	1	—
Gond	1	—	1	—
Baraik	17	3	14	—
Goswami	5	1	4	—
Saosi	5	—	5	—
Bairagi	2	1	1	—
Goala	4	—	4	—
Malpahari	10	—	10	—
Mahali	7	1	6	—
Bhokta	4	2	2	—
Ghasi	19	5	14	—
Korowa	6	1	5	—
Routia	1	—	1	—
Bhuiyan	1	—	—	1
Lohar	6	1	5	—
Turi	4	—	3	1
Ore	1	—	1	—
Castes				
Bengali	1	—	—	1
Bihari	9	2	6	1
Nepali	20	4	16	—
Total	276 (100.00)	60 (21.74)	208 (75.36)	8 (2.90)

It is revealed from the above table that majority of the households are of nuclear type. Out of the total workers' households of 276 there are 208 (75.36 per cent) nuclear families. The nuclear families comprise of parents and unmarried children. There are 8 other households which are the residual form of nuclear families and may be categorised as unclassified. Five of these households have single member of each. The other three households have two members of each. One of them is comprised of two brothers; other is comprised of a brother and a sister; and the third is comprised of a boy with his father's sister. The joint families include married couples, unmarried and married children along with their relatives.

Nuclear family is commonly found in any industrial society. Similarly, in the plantation, workers prefer to live in the nuclear families. The plantation system also influences the workers to live in the nuclear families, because the houses which are provided to them are suitable for nuclear family. Besides, there are other facilities which encourage nuclearisation of the workers' families in the plantation.[12] However, these we will discuss in some details in Chapter 5.

Literacy

The plantation workers of Chandmoni Tea Estate as well as of other plantations in Dooars and Terai are mostly Adivasi origin. Most of them are traditionally agriculturists and illiterate. Today even most of the women workers are illiterate and only a few have primary education. Out of total population of 1,252, 815 (65.09 per cent) are illiterate of whom 382 (30.51 per cent) are men and 433 (34.58 per cent) are women. There are 203 children under 6 years of age who are automatically excluded from the sample. The rest 234 persons (18.69 per cent) are only literate of whom 187 (14.94 per cent) are men and 47 (3.75 per cent) are women. Out of 187 literate men only 108 (8.63 per cent) have primary education and 79 (6.31 per cent) have secondary education (Table 18). Out of 47 literate women 38 (3.04 per cent) have primary education and 9 (0.72 per cent) have secondary education. The number of literates among the Adivasis are 179 of which 142 (12.93 per cent) are men and 37 (3.36 per cent) are women. In case of non-Adivasis the number of literate men are 45 (29.22 per cent) and literate women are 10 (6.49 per cent). Among the 142 literate Adivasi men only 94 (66.19 per cent) have primary education and only 48 (33.8 per cent) have secondary education but none of them are matriculate. In case of 37 literate Adivasi women only 30 (81.08 per cent) have primary education and 7 (18.91 per cent) have secondary education. None of the women are matriculate. Among the 45 non-Adivasi literate men only 14 (31.11 per cent) have primary education and 31 (68.88 per cent) have secondary education of whom only 3 (6.6 per cent) are matriculates. In case of 10 non-Adivasi literate women 8 (80.0 per cent) have primary education and only 2 (20.00 per cent) have secondary education without a matriculation degree.

From the above discussion it is observed that workers with higher education are generally from the male and non-Adivasi groups. Such educated persons are from the present generation and they are mostly employed in Railways and Military services.

Table 18

Ethnic Groups and Literacy

(Persons included above 6 years of age)

Ethnic Group	Number of Literate Persons: Primary M	Primary F	Secondary M	Secondary F	Total	%	Number of Illiterate Persons: M	F	Total	%	Persons Under 6 years
Adivasis											
Oraon	34	13	25	4	76	32.67	131	137	268	32.88	84
Munda	19	10	16	-	45	19.23	73	85	158	19.38	43
Kheria	1	2	4	2	9	3.84	12	13	25	3.05	2
Meher	-	-	-	-	-	-	5	4	9	1.10	1
Gond	-	-	-	-	-	-	3	1	4	0.49	-
Baraik	12	3	1	-	16	6.83	23	24	47	5.76	5
Goswami	3	1	1	-	5	2.13	3	5	8	0.98	4
Saosi	1	-	-	-	1	0.42	5	9	14	1.71	2
Bairagi	2	-	-	-	2	0.85	2	4	6	0.73	2
Goala	1	-	-	-	1	0.42	5	2	7	0.85	-
Malpahari	1	-	-	-	1	0.42	12	16	28	3.43	8
Mahali	3	-	-	-	3	1.28	10	13	23	2.82	6
Bhokta	2	-	-	1	3	1.28	3	9	12	1.47	2
Ghasi	12	1	1	-	14	5.98	29	28	57	8.99	15
Korowa	-	-	-	-	-	-	11	11	22	2.69	5
Routia	-	-	-	-	-	-	3	2	5	0.61	-
Bhuiyan	-	-	-	-	-	-	1	-	1	0.12	-
Lohar	1	-	-	-	1	0.42	13	15	28	3.43	3
Turi	2	-	-	-	2	0.85	5	4	9	1.10	3
Ore	-	-	-	-	-	-	2	1	3	0.36	-
Castes											
Bengali	-	-	1	-	1	0.42	-	-	-	-	-
Bihari	1	-	9	-	10	4.27	11	13	24	2.94	3
Nepali	13	8	21	2	44	18.80	20	37	57	6.99	15
Total	108	38	79	9	234	100.00	382	433	815	100.00	203

M.B. M for male and F for female.

The rate of female education is very low in this plantation. Among the Adivasis the Christians are more educated than the Saonsars (non-Christians professing tribal religion). Though there is a primary school run by the plantation authority, most of the students are outsiders. Proportion of the students belonging to the families of plantation workers is very low. The Christian workers prefer to send their children to the nearby Missionary schools. Four Oraon families have sent their sons to a boarding school. The Christians, in general, appear to be more eager to educate their children than the non-Christian Adivasis.

Religion

The majority of the Adivasis of the tea plantation still adhere to their own traditional religion. They are locally known as Saonsars. Religious conversion has recently appeared as an important phenomenon among the plantation workers belonging to various Adivasi groups. Christianity has considerably affected the Adivasi religion. Compared to this, Hinduisation is not prominent among them as the process of conversion is very slow. It might take several generations to become Hindus. In West Bengal and Christian plantation workers are nearly ten per cent of the total plantation workers. They belong to the Roman Catholic and Protestant sects. However, Christian Adivasi workers of Chandmoni Tea Estate belong to Roman Catholic sect only. The Adivasi plantation workers of Chandmoni Tea Estate can broadly be divided into two religions groups, namely, the Adivasi Saonsars (76.42 per cent) and the Adivasi Christians (23.57 per cent). The Saonsars are actually those Adivasis who profess their traditional religion.

Christianity has affected Oraons, Mundas and Kherias of Chandmoni plantation. But the conversion mainly took place one or two generations ago, except a few who have recently converted themselves under the influence of the Christian Mission or through marriage with the Christians. Christianity is found to a large extend among the Oraons than among other Adivasi workers of the region. In this plantation out of 90 families of the Oraons 49 (54.44 per cent) are followers of Christianity and 41 (45.55 per cent) are Saonsar (Table 19). The Mundas and Kherias in this plantation show less Christianity as out of

53 families of the Mundas only 6 (11.32 per cent) are Saonsars, and of 8 Kheria families 3 (37.5 per cent) are Christians and 5 (62.5 per cent) are Saonsars.

Table 19

Ethnicity and Religion of the Adivasi Workers

Ethnic Group	Total Number of Households	Number of Households	
		Adivasi-Saonsar	Adivasi-Christian
Oraon	90	41	49
Munda	53	47	6
Kheria	8	5	3
Meher	2	2	-
Gond	1	1	-
Baraik	17	17	-
Goswami	5	5	-
Saosi	5	5	-
Bairagi	2	2	-
Goala	4	4	-
Malpahari	10	10	-
Mahali	7	7	-
Bhokta	4	4	-
Ghasi	19	19	-
Korowa	6	6	-
Routia	1	1	-
Bhuiyan	1	1	-
Lohar	6	6	-
Turi	4	4	-
Ore	1	1	-
Total	246 (100.00)	188 (76.42)	58 (23.58)

A few Adivasis have adopted some Hindu rituals and customs. They are Goswamis, Bairagis, Goala and Bhoktas having a total household of 13. There are a few castes of Bengali, Bihari and Nepali communities who are Hindus. Altogether they constitute 30 (10.87 per cent) households.

Migration

Tea plantation was always associated with a resident labour

force who were originally slave labourers or indentured labourers. At the beginning of tea plantations in the state much difficulty was faced in the recruitment of labourers from among the indigenous people. To meet the labour crisis a large number of Adivasi people were brought from Bihar, Madhya Pradesh, Orissa and from within West Bengal. Almost the entire labour force in tea plantations of Terai of Darjeeling district and Dooars of Jalpaiguri district consisted of immigrant labourers and their descendants. Under the Amendment Act of 1870 the Sardari system of recruitment was introduced. From that time till 1952 both Sardari system and Arkatti (licensed recruiter) system of recruitment were in vogue.[13] Since 1952 there has been no recruitment in plantations at least officially through this system. However, the system of recruitment will be discussed in some details in the next chapter.

Immigration of tea labourers was considerably high in West Bengal between 1860 and 1881. In Terai the first garden was established in 1862 and other gardens were opened by 1866. Between 1896 and 1901 tea price fell greatly in Britain. Consequently a number of gardens reduced their labour force. During 1901 to 1911 the plantation population showed a decline in its number.[14] Migration to the tea gardens of the state was mainly family based. The nature of the tea industry required both men and women labourers. At the same time the planters wanted cheap labour. So they encouraged families to migrate from different parts of the country, specially from Chotanagpur and to settle permanently in the tea gardens. Thus the Adivasi families from Bihar, Orissa, Madhya Pradesh form a new settlement in plantations.

In Chandmoni Tea Estate, workers belong to various ethnic groups who are not indigenous people. During the fieldwork it has been found that out of total population of 1,252 only 461 (36.82 per cent) persons have immigrated from different places. The rest of the population, i.e., 791 (63.17 per cent) persons are born in Chandmoni whose forefathers had immigrated one or two generations ago. In Chandmoni 405 persons (36.88 per cent), out of the total Adivasi population of 1,098, are the immigrants from Bihar, Orissa, Madhya Pradesh and other parts of West Bengal. Fifty six persons, i.e., 36.36 per cent,

Table 20

Adivasi and Non-Adivasi Migration in Chandmoni Tea Estate

Ethnic Group	Number of Migrants from Outside West Bengal by Contract		Number of Migrants from Other Plantations		Number of Migrants from Villages of West Bengal		Number of Migrants from Outside West Bengal		Total Number of Migrants	Persons Born in Chandmoni	Total Population of Chandimoni
	M %	F %	M %	F %	M %	F %	M %	F %	%	%	%
Adivasi	59 5.37	34 3.09	63 5.73	107 9.74	22 2.00	40 3.64	39 3.55	41 3.73	405 36.88	693 63.11	1,098 100.00
Non-Adivasi	-	-	-	-	2 1.29	11 7.14	24 15.58	19 12.33	56 36.36	98 63.64	154 100.00
Total	59 4.71	34 2.71	63 5.03	107 8.54	24 1.91	51 4.07	63 5.03	60 4.79	461 36.82	761 63.18	1,252 100.00

N.B. M for male & F for female.

of the 154 non-Adivasis are migrants from Bangladesh, Bihar and Nepal (Table 20).

In the present population structure of Chandmoni the Adivasi labourers recruited through the Sardari system are very few. The total number of immigrants recruited directly through this system is 93 (8.46 per cent) of which 59 (5.37 per cent) are male and 34 (3.09 per cent) are female. As Chandmoni plantation was established in 1922 recruitment through this system was not very necessary because already at that time there were surplus labourers in the tea plantations of West Bengal. It is needless to say that the surplus labourers were either immigrants or their descendants. In Chandmoni no non-Adivasis were recruited through this system as most of them came after Independence.

During the pre-Independence period inter-garden labour movement was very high. The surplus labourers in the plantations encouraged inter-garden movement of the labourers to a considerable extent. In Chandmoni 170 (15. 48 per cent) persons belonging to the different Adivasi groups have come from other gardens and settled either as workers or as their permanent dependants. Out of 170 such workers there are 63 (5.73 per cent) men and 107 (9.74 per cent) women. It has been noticed that movement of Adivasi workers from other gardens has taken place mainly due to marriage. Out of 107 women, 74 (69.15 per cent) have come to this garden to live with their husbands after marriage. Only 8 (12.69 per cent) men are found to have shifted to this garden after their marriage with girls belonging to this garden. It is important to note that while females are moving to this garden through marriage the male also show the similar trend of movement though at a lower scale, into this garden. In respect of the latter group it is particularly due to the higher incidence of Ghar-damad customs among the Ghasis and Baraiks where a man after marriage takes up residence with his father-in law. No inter-garden movement has occurred among the non-Adivasis on such a ground.

About 123 (9.82 per cent) persons have come to this garden from various places, namely, Bihar, Madhya Pradesh, Nepal and Bangladesh. Of 123 persons there are 63 men and 60 women, and 80 belong to the different Adivasi communities and 43 to the non-Adivasi communities. Most of the immigrated non-Adivasis have come from Nepal and Bihar. Only 1 Bengali male has come from Bangladesh. This immigrant population has either come to this garden itself in search of jobs as workers or as the permanent dependants of the workers. Their recruitment has taken place directly by the garden authority. They were not brought through the Sardari or Arkatti system.

There are other groups of workers belonging to Adivasi and non-Adivasi groups who have come from several villages of West Bengal. But they are not the indigenous population of West Bengal. Their forefathers had immigrated to West Bengal one or two generations ago from Bihar and Nepal and settled down in different villages. Altogether they are 75 (5.99 per cent) in number (24 male and 51 female). There are 62 Adivasis and 13 non-Adivasis among these immigrant labourers. Some of them are recruited in this plantation directly by the garden authority and others have come as permanent dependants of workers already employed in the garden.

Before 1952 the migration took place in an organised way. But in the post-Independence period there is no such organised migration. One cannot give the exact date when the migration of the workers in Terai plantation has actually stopped. According to Indian Tea Association (ITA) and Indian Tea Planters Association (ITPA) reports there has been no direct recruitment of workers since 1952. As the formation of labour unions have taken place in every garden after 1952 all the recruitments are now made through the unions from the bonafide dependants of the workers.

BUREAUCRACY IN TEA INDUSTRY

Like any well organised industry a plantation has also an organisation of work and a hierarchy of staff. The organisation of work includes distribution of work among the various categories of staff, keeping attendance registrar, paying salaries and ration and doing other types of work. The hierarchy of staff includes all types of employees of the plantation right from the manager to the wage labourers. All the employees could be differentiated into four categories, namely, (*i*) Managerial staff, (*ii*) Office-staff, (*iii*) sub-staff and (*iv*) Workers.. This staffing pattern is mainly found among the plantations run by Indian owners.

Chandmoni Tea Estate is owned by a public limited company. All the responsibilities of this company are vested in a manager. There are four managerial staff of which manager occupies the top position in the plantation hierarchy. Below the manager there are two assistant managers and one medical officer. In the plantation hierarchy the medical officer also occupies a position in the managerial staff. In the history of plantation no women has ever been appointed to occupy a position in the managerial category. So also in Chandmoni Tea Estate all the four managerial staff are males.

Below the category of the managerial staff there is a category of staff consisting of seventeen minor officials. Two of them are garden supervisors (Bagan Babu), one each is a factory supervisor (Factory Babu) and a pharmacist (Davawallo), a driver, a fitter, an engine driver and rest are clerks in the office. Out of 17 staff members of this category only one is a woman who works as a clerk in the office. The categories of the managerial and office staff consist of Bengalis with the exception of a Bihari who is employed as a clerk.

In Chandmoni there are 55 sub-staff members who are just below the category of the staff in the plantation hierarchy. They are mainly from among the Adivasi groups which contribute 46 sub-staff members. Among the Adivasi sub-staff Oraons, Mundas and Baraiks provide the majority while there is none of this category from the Goswamis, Saosis, Korawas, Ores, Turis, Majis, Mehers and Gonds. Besides, 12 sub-staff members belong to the Bengali, Bihari and Nepali caste groups. The Bihari sub-staff belong to Brahmin, Rout and Khusbaha castes; the Nepali sub-staff belong to the Chhetri caste while the Bengali sub-staff belong to the Brahmin caste (Table 21 and 22).

The category of the sub-staff consists of junior supervisory staff and non-supervisory staff (Table 21). Among the junior supervisory staff there are Munsis (field supervisor), whose position in the hierarchy is higher than that of the garden labourers. Next to the Munsi there are Chaprasis. Both Munsi and Chaprasi supervise the works of the other sub-staff below them. In Chandmoni there are only 1 Munsi and 1 Chaprasi.

Next in the hierarchy there are Boidars who keep attendance

of the workers and the sub-staff who are engaged in the field. there is one Boidar for the men workers and another Boidar for the women workers.

Dafadars and Sardars come next to the Boidars who mainly supervise fieldwork of the workers. According to the order of the assistant managers or garden Babu they assign work to the workers, supervise directly on the spot, guide them in the action, and if necessary show the actual action of work in practice. Munsis and Chaparasis also order them for the work to be done. Sardars' position as well as duties are similar to that of Dafadars. Both of them are involved to check the quality of the work of the labourers when they are in cultivation work. The Dafadar guides the workers along with the correct lines (Mela). In Chandmoni there are 6 Dafadars and 12 Sardars.

Table 21

Sub-Staff Workers of Chandmoni Tea Estate, 1978-79

	Local Categories	Number	Ethnic Group
1.	Munshi (Junior Supervisor Grade I)	1	Nepali-1
2.	Chaprasi (Junior Supervisor Grade II)	1	Oraon-1
3.	Boidar (Workers' Attendance Keeper)	2	Munda-1 Ghasi-1
4.	Dafadar (Field Supervisor)	6	Mahali-1 Malpahari-1 Bairagi-1 Baraik-1 Oraon-2
5.	Sardar (Block Leader)	12	Lohar-1 Bhokta-1 Nepali-1 Munda-4 Baraik-2 Oraon-3
6.	Chowkidar (Watchman)	18	Oraon-5 Baraik-2 Nepali-2

			Bihari-6
			Munda-3
7.	Peon	1	Oraon-1
8.	Paniwalla (Water carrier)	7	Bhuiyan-1
			Ghasi-2
			Kheria-1
			Oraon-1
			Munda-2
9.	Davawalla (Health assistant)		Kheria-1
10.	Factory worker-Skilled and Unskilled	5	Bengali-1
			Munda-3
			Baraik-1
11.	Mistri (Carpenter)	1	Bihari-1

Next position is occupied by Chowkidars, Peons and Paniwallas whose duties are to keep a watch on the plantation properties, bringing letters from the post-office and to carry water to the field while the workers are on duty respectively. There are 18 Chowkidars, 1 Peon and 7 Paniwallas in Chandmoni. Paniwalla also carries water for every households of the managerial and other staff. Besides, 1 Davawalla (health assistant), 5 factory workers and 1 carpenter are employed as sub-staff.

The sub-staff of Chandmoni Tea Estate are always drawing better wages than that of ordinary workers and are also given some additional facilities.

While the office-staff are recruited from both men and women, sub-staff are exclusively from men. This is because the plantation authority likes to recruit men only for these positions, who they think can effectively command over the workers in the garden. Moreover, the nature of duties of the supervisory and non-supervisory workers in the garden are considered unsuitable for the women. The sub-staff are generally promoted from the ordinary workers and only men workers are considered eligible for such promotions. Women workers are deprived of such promotion opportunities. The sub-staff are considered positionally higher than the ordinary workers, and they receive a fixed monthly wage. The workers get daily wage.

The workers play the most important role in the production system and they form the totality of the labour force in the plantation. They are commonly referred to as 'Coolies' in the plantation societies of West Bengal and Assam. They directly involve themselves in the production. They do all types of manual labours, i.e; plucking, hoeing, clearing weeds, pruning, etc. In this sense they are the actual producers in the mode of production of the plantation system who sell their labour power and earn their livelihood. Except the workers the rest of the persons in the plantation are not directly involved in the various production process.

Generally in a tea plantation there are two types of workers who can be separated on the basis of the mode of payment of their wages. One of the types is the daily rated and other is the monthly-rated workers. All the monthly rated workers are considered slightly superior to the ordinary workers as they get a little higher monthly wages. However, only the men can occupy this position and women are not considered eligible. The daily rated workers are ordinary workers appointed on daily wages. The monthly and daily wages of the workers will be discussed in some details in the following chapter. The daily rated workers are more important for tea production in a plantation. This category of plantation workers is also generally grouped by the management into male, female and children. Only in this category of workers women are employed. In Chandmoni Tea Estate there are 203 male, 221 female and 36 child workers who are paid daily wages (Table 22). There are only 55 males who are paid monthly wages. None of the females and children are monthly rated. Both male and female groups of workers belong to the age group of 18 years and above. Child workers belong to the age group of 12 to 16 years. They get lesser wages than the adult men and women workers. Upto 1979 there was another category of workers consisting of both men and women who occupied a position in between adult and children workers. They were known in the plantation as 'adolescent' workers who belonged to the age group of 16-18 years. They received lower wages than those of the adult men workers, but equal to the wages of the women workers. In October 1975 Equal Remuneration Act was passed which sought to remove wage differences between the sexes. Thus there is equal wage for men and women workers. Previously the work load and wages of adolescent workers were same as female workers. After 1978 the adolescent category of workers was abolished. However, in Chandmoni

Tea Estate there are only three categories of workers—men, women and children.

Table 22

Men, Women and Children Workers Including Monthly Rated Sub-Staff in 1978-79

Adivasi/ Caste	Man Monthly Rated	Man Daily Rated	Women Daily Rated	Children Daily Rated	Total
Adivasis					
Oraon	13	71	80	12	176
Munda	13	40	47	6	106
Kheria	2	5	5	2	14
Meher	-	1	1	1	3
Gond	-	1	1	-	2
Baraik	6	13	11	3	33
Goswami	-	4	4	1	9
Saosi	-	4	4	-	8
Bairagi	1	2	2	-	5
Goala	-	3	2	-	5
Malpahari	1	7	9	1	18
Mahali	1	5	6	1	13
Bhokta	1	1	3	-	5
Ghasi	3	14	14	3	34
Korowa	-	5	5	-	10
Routia	-	1	2	-	3
Bhuiyan	1	-	-	-	1
Lohar	1	5	6	-	12
Turi	-	3	2	-	5
Ore	-	1	1	-	2
Castes					
Bengali	1		-	-	1
Bihari	7	5	2	1	1
Nepali	4	12	14	5	35
	55	203	221	36	515
Total	10.68	36.42	42.91	6.99	100.00

References

1. Gait, E., *A History of Assam,* Thacker Spink & Co, Calcutta, 1935, pp. 411-412.

2. Dash, A.J., *Bengal Gazetteers,* Darjeeling, 1947, p. 113.
3. Ibid., p. 114.
4. Ibid., p. 119.
5. Griffiths, P, *The History of Indian Tea Industry,* Weidenfel and Nicolson, London. 1967, p. 30.
6. Bhowmik, S.K., "Recruitment Policy of Tea Plantations" in *North-East Quarterly, Vol. I,* No. 2, 1982.
7. Dash, A.J., op. cit., p. 115.
8. Hunter, W.W., *A Statistical Account of Bengal,* Vol. X (Re-printed), D.K. Publishing House, New Delhi, 1974, pp. 166-172.
9. Ibid., pp. 164-165.
10. Dash, A.J., op.cit., p. 119.
11. *Tea Statistics, 1978-79,* Tea Board of India, Calcutta, pp. 110-111.
12. Bhowmik, S. *Class Fomation in the Plantation System,* People's Publishing House, New Delhi, 1981, pp. 116-117.
13. For the nature of Sardari and Arkatti recruitment see A. Guha, *Planter-Raj to Swaraj,* ICHR, New Delhi, 1977, pp. 17-18.
14. *Census of India,* 1961, West Bengal, District Census Handbook, Darjeeling, p. 24.

Chapter 4

Women as Plantation Workers

This chapter deals with the working life of the women workers of the Chandmoni Tea Estate. Here we will discuss women as plantation workers, their traditional occupational background, process of their recruitment in the plantation, nature of plantation work they perform, wages and other occupational facilities which they enjoy, their attitudes toward the plantation work and commitment, their participation in the trade unions and relations with the management, etc. All these will help us in understanding the women as plantation workers and nature of their adjustment to the working environment of this agro-industry.

OCCUPATIONAL BACKGROUND

Traditional Occupation of the Workers

Tea plantation is an agro-industry where both agricultural and industrial working environment exist. In such an industry recruitment of labourers was largely made, particularly in the plantations of Assam and Dooars and Terai regions of West Bengal, from Adivasis of the neighbouring states. Most of these Adivasis were proverty-stricken illiterate villagers who had no experience of industrial occupation. There were also a few Hindus among the early recruits who were equality poor and ignorant. As tea industry is agro-based and located in rural areas workers with rural background are expected to adapt better with the working environment of the industry with a consequent effect upon lessening the conflict between home life and working life. Naturally the question of adaptation of women workers to this industry is a major concern of this thesis which will be examined in detail in subsequent chapters.

The tea plantation workers generally have an agricultural background. Though they are considered as industrial workers they have vast differences with the other industrial workers in India. The latter group of workers generally occupy a working status which is considered as superior to those of the former. The plantation workers generally differ from the population of surrounding regions also. Almost in all plantations the workers live in semi-isolation from the outside world. This was more true in earlier times than it is today. Since the passing of the Plantation Labour Act in 1951 the contact of the plantation workers with the outside world has considerably increased, yet, by and large, socially they move within the framework of their plantation society. This feature, together with the preponderence of Adivasi workers, has given a special character to the plantation workers not found elsewhere in other industries. In Chandmoni Tea Estate out of 515 workers 464, i.e., 90.10 per cent are non-Hindu Adivasis and only 51 workers, i.e., 9.90 per cent belong to Hindu caste groups. Among the women workers 205 out of 221, i.e., 92.7 per cent hail from Adivasi communities and the rest 16, i.e., 7.3 per cent are Hindu castes. From this it appears that when the plantation had begun its expansion programme a higher proportion of Adivasis instead of Hindu estates were attracted to this type of industry. As tea industry requires no previous work experience and education both men and women are admirably suited for it particularly for the various types of garden work. However, there is no significant difference between Hindu and non-Hindu Adivasi workers in terms of their industrial background and level of education.

Employment of women and children in large number is a striking feature of all tea plantations. In fact, the unit of recruitment is the family. All members of a family—men, women and children—are provided with work. In proportion to men, women are generally employed in larger number in tea plantations, as has been pointed earlier, than any other organised industry. Being akin to agriculture, plantation work and its environment seem to be more congenial to women than that in a factory or a mine.

The bulk of the Adivasi wokers in Dooars and Terai plantations are descendants of the Adivasi immigrants from Chotanagpur.

They form, more or less homogenous group despite their different Adivasi origin. They are commonly referred to as Madesia. The plantation workers of non-Adivasi origin are drawn from various Nepali and Bihari caste groups.

In regard to the traditional occupations of the plantation workers two occupational groups may be found: agriculturists and non-agriculturists. Agriculture was the traditional occupation of the Oraons, Mundas and Kherias. Among these plantation workers it is a feature that the cultivating communities consider themselves superior to those of the non-cultivating groups.[1]

The traditional occupation of the Oraons is agriculture. The Oraons consider it derogatory to engage themselves in occupations such as weaving, basketry or wicker work, pottery and working in iron. They necessarily require the services of other tribes and castes to supply their few needs. Loharas make plough-shares and other tools and implements; Baraiks generally weave clothes; Turis, Mahalis and Ores weave or plait baskets; and Ghasis play music at the social festivals of these Adivasi communities. Besides, there are few other Adivasis living side by side with the Oraons. They are Mundas, Kherias, Korwas and Asurs. The Mundas and Kherias stand on the same level of culture as the Oraons.[2] These three Adivasis are traditionally agriculturists while the rest of the communities are non-agriculturists.

Among the Adivasi population of the tea plantation there exists a system of occupational hierarchy which plays an important role in their social life. Such a hierarchy seems to have given rise to a superior-inferior complex which determines the pattern of day to day social interactions. The traditionally cultivating Adivasis of Chotanagpur consider themselves superior to the non-cultivating Adivasis and scheduled castes. These superior groups do not interdine with the inferior groups. The Oraons, Mundas and Kherias being agriculturists consider themselves superior to the other non-cultivating and scheduled castes who render various services to them. The former have communal relations among themselves but do not interdine with the latter.

Among the Hindus there are Bengalis, Biharis and Nepalis. There is one Bengali Brahmin whose traditional occupation was priesthood. Biharis have a few caste groups in this plantation. Among them there are four Brahmin families, one each of the

Kurmi, Khusbaha, Routh, Hazam and Muchi. Traditionally the Brahmins are priests, the Kurmis and Khusbahas are agriculturists, Rouths live on trading and Hazams are barbers and Muchis are shoe makers. Generally women of the Bengali and most Bihari castes do not participate in their economic activities which are essentially the work of menfolks. Most of the Nepalis are traditionally agriculturists except a few like Kamis (blacksmith) and Thamis who were traditionally the traders.

In the Nepali community the Brahmins occupy the highest position in the caste hierarchy, and along with the Chhetris they form a bulk of the influential and wealthy people of Nepal. The main occupation of the Brahmins and Chhetris is farming and government services. The Brahmins also act as family priests. Like all other agriculturists, the Chhetris also mainly live in rural areas of Nepal. Majority of the Chhetris are farmers. Pradhans are one of the groups of the Newar caste system. They belong to Shrestha caste who are traditionally merchants. The Rais are commonly known as the Kiranti people of East Nepal. They cultivate both dry and wet fields. In addition, they grow various types of vegetables. The Rai women take part in agricultural operations. But among the Brahmins, Chhetris, Pradhans, Kamis the Thamis women usually do not take part in agricultural operations. The Pradhans, Kamis and Thamis are traditionally merchants, blacksmiths and traders respectively.[3]

It is, therefore, seen that most of the Adivasi women who form the bulk of the female work force of the plantation are with an agricultural background. Comparatively, the Hindu caste women who are not from the agricultural castes have joined the work force in a much smaller number. Only in the recent years there has developed a tendency among these women to accept a job in the plantation, if available. This is obviously due to "dire economic needs" as some of them told me.

A striking feature of the labour force in this plantation, as elsewhere, is that employment of women and men is almost equal in number. The reasons are : (i) recruitment of workers is generally on family basis, (ii) plucking is more efficiently done by women workers as it is similar to those of agriculture and women workers mostly hail from rural areas who do not feel any difficulty in this work and (iii) migration of workers with their families creates obligations to the management to provide wage work to the family members of the workers.

Recruitment of Women Workers in Plantations

It has already been mentioned that both men and women are recruited more or less in equal proportion in tea plantations. The recruitment policy in plantation does not follow any disparity in recruiting men and women workers. However, recruitment of women workers is a part of general recruitment process which has deep historical roots. We will briefly mention this process below.

At the beginning of tea plantations the employers had to depend entirely on various sources and agencies for the recruitment of workers. There were some recruiting agents in Assam, Sardars were in north-east India except Assam, and Kanganies were in South India.[4] Though origin of tea plantation labourers of Assam and West Bengal, except the hills of Darjeeling district, was same the process of recruitment in the latter region differed from that of the former. Tea industry in Assam started in 1839 while in Terai and Dooars of West Bengal it started in 1866 and 1874 respectively. The planters of Terai and Dooars had the knowledge of labour recruitment process of Assam, and they could avoid the serious mistakes committed by the employers in Assam.

There was acute shortage and unsatisfactory character of local labourers in Assam plantations in 1839. In 1841 the Assam Tea Company first attempted to import labourers from the tribal belt of Chotanagpur. In 1859 the Tea Planters Association was formed to regulate the recruitment process of tea labourers in Assam in an organised manner.[5] Recruitment was done mainly through the Arkattis who employed dubious means to recruit the simple tribals. The Arkattis were mainly from Baraiks and Ghasis who were landless craftsmen living in the neighbouring regions of the tribals like Oraons, Mundas, Santals and Kherias. Sometimes the Arkattis were Hindus and Muslims also. The hard working, poverty stricken tribals of Chotanagpur were suitable for tea gardens as they were also the cheapest labourers available to the employers.[6]

However, recruitment through contractors in 1863 was

unsatisfactory. Recruitment was also done through the graden authorities themselves. This was often done through the garden Sardars, who were often sent to the recruiting districts.[7] These two methods of recruitment of labourers through Arkattis and through garden Sardars were often followed by the plantation owners for collecting labourers. The Sardars of the gardens were sent to the recruitment ground in the recruiting season (generally began after the rains in October and ended in February). It was easier for the Sardars to induce the new recruits to show the advantages of work and the prospects of ultimate settlement on independent holdings. The Sardars would look around among his countrymen for anyone willing to go to "Bhutan" for work. After collecting a few they would take them to the recruiting agents who would advance them the necessary money to return with the coolies. The Sardars were usually accompanied by a garden supervisor who always kept an eye over them.[8]

The recruited labourers were then sent to various tea plantations in an inhuman condition. Basic health and sanitation facilities were not provided to them. Thus a few of them survived. This proved expensive for the planters and the Workmen's Breach of Contract (Act No. XVII) Act was passed in 1859. This act rendered the labourers liable for prosecution for any break of contact and they had to sign a bond for working in the tea garden for specific time period. In 1861 the government appointed a committee for enquiry into the migration of labourers to Assam and Cachar.[9] The result of which was the passing of Inland Emigration Act in 1863. That was amended in 1865, permitting a few concessions to the plantation workers like reducing their contract period into three years from indefinite period and giving some kind of protection to them.[10]

Dooars was annexed from Bhutan in 1865 and European planters found a new tea-growing region there. In 1874 Assam was separated from Bengal. In the Darjeeling hills no recruitment problem existed. Population of Nepal was rising rapidly and the economic pressure forced them to come out. Thus a good number of Nepalis were compelled to migrate from Nepal and settled in Darjeeling district, and gardens of this district recruited all these labourers without formalities. In the Terai region tea cultivation was expanding very rapidly, and though upto 1873 there had been no importation of labourers the demand for labourers was just beginning to exceed supply.[11]

There were 56 gardens in Darjeeling district in 1870, 44 gardens in hills and 12 in Terai having a total labour force of 8,347. After four years the number of gardens increased to 113 and the number of labourers increased to 19,424.[12]

Labourers in the Terai and Dooars plantations were always 'free' in the sense that they were not put under any kind of contract and could leave at their will. One of the reasons may be that the planters of Terai and Dooars had the advantage of knowing the recruitment system of tea labourers in Assam and could avoid the mistakes committed by them. In Terai and Dooars three types of recruitment system were prevalent. The most popular was the Sardari system and other was Arkatti system. The third one was the recruitment through local agents of some private agencies in the recruiting districts. The manager of the garden generally sent a Babu (clerk) to the recruiting areas who contacted these agencies and selected the workers. These agencies made some agreements with the labourers and the garden concerned. The workers were given various false promises by the recruiter that the labourers would be given light work and plenty of paddy land in the garden. The planters also recruited annually unindentured labourers from Chotanagpur, Santal Parganas, Chaibasa and from the neighbouring regions through the garden Sardars. In order to recruit labourers, the planters had established an organisation called the Tea Districts Labour Association with the headquarters in Calcutta. The machinery of recruitment and forwarding was provided by this association which also recruited on behalf of its members for the Dooars and Terai plantations in Bengal though no legislation to this effect existed in the state. Seventy seven per cent of the tea industry in north-east india recruited labourers through this association.[13] The Tea District Labour Association had its recruiting agents in the recruiting districts and to whom the Sardars would report for assistance.

Thus the recruitment was carried out through the recruiters who were known as Garden Sardars, Resident Sardars and Local Recruiters. The first two worked as the agents of the tea estates from which they had been sent to recruit, while the recruiters were agents of the Tea District Labour Association.

The Christian missionaries had their own Labour Bureau, Catholic Labour Bureau at Ranchi, to help the Tea District Labour Association who also took a share as recruiting fees for their funds. Thus in Dooars the permanent labour force grew from nearly 103,000 in 1913 to 150,000 in 1919.[14]

Assam, Dooars and Terai might differ in method of recruitment but in both cases there was the problem of labour enticement. The employers who had less labourers would seek to entice labourers from their neighbouring gardens and they had spent considerable amount for it. The recruited labourers were usually given a few rupees in advance. The cost of recruitment for workers from Chotanagpur and Santal Parganas in 1944 was twenty five rupees per head before the Second World War and thirty six rupees per head after the War. The Sardar's commission was three rupees per recruited worker.[15]

In 1889 a somewhat elaborate set of rules provided interalia that workers leaving one estate for another without permission must be turned out or sent back. Sixty five per cent of the gardens in the membership of Dooars Planters Association signed the agreement. In 1920 a reciprocal arrangement was made with the Terai Gardens which had its own rules since 1908.[16] In 1959 recruitment from outside West Bengal and Assam had been reduced and the Tea District Labour Association was dissolved.

It was found that in north-east India there was no longer the problem of shortage of labour. There is now an almost settled labour force in the area and instead of sending agents to distant places the employers could recruit workers directly. In fact there was some pockets of surplus labour force. The Nineth session of the Industrial Committee on Plantations reviewed the policy of recruitment of labourers for Assam tea gardens in August, 1960 and decided that no fresh recruitment should be made from outside Assam except with the permission of the government and that movement of labourers from surplus to deficit areas within Assam should be encouraged with the help of special Employment Exchange. In other cases, tea estates recruited relatives of their workers or engaged ordinary-labourers from adjoining villages to cope with the rush of work.

In the Terai region a few gardens recruited their labourers through the Tea District Labour Association but in most cases recruitment was mainly through the Sardars or through some private agencies or through the families already employed in the gardens. A major portion of such labourers were the migrants from Chotanagpur and Santal Parganas. Others were the local labourers or the migrants from Nepal.

Recruitment in Chandmoni Tea Estate

It has already been mentioned that the Chandmoni plantation is located in the Terai region of Darjeeling district. Therefore, recruitment system in this plantation conforms to that of the Terai region and slightly differs from that of the Dooars region. In Chandmoni labourers were originally from Chotanagpur and Santal Parganas of Bihar, Madhya Pradesh, Orissa and Nepal. A significant portion of them consists of non-Hindu Adivasis like Oraon, Munda, Kheria, Malpahari, Korowa, Lohar, Baraik, Ghasi, Mahali, Turi and Bhokta.

Recruitment of workers in this plantation during the pre-independence period was done mainly through the Sardars. Only a few recruitments were done through some private agencies. Migration to this garden was primarily family based. Before 1940 when there was labour scarcity both husband and wife were recruited together as workers. That time this plantation preferred to recruit couples from various Adivasi societies as they were easily available on low wages. However, some individual labourers were recruited also who had come in quest of plantation jobs or who had come to this garden as wives of the workers. Christian Churches played an important role in the labour recruitment process. The bulk of the Christian labourers had already been converted to Christianity in their native places and they were advised by their Church authority to migrate to the tea districts for jobs. A Roman Catholic Church was established in 1891 in Mallaguri which is very near to Chandmoni Tea Estate. This Church had a direct role in the supply of labourers in Chandmoni.

Some of the labourers of Chandmoni had previously worked in other plantations of Dooars who came here for better wages and facilities as there was disparity in wages in Dooars and Terai. Some women who came to Chandmoni from other plantations through marriages were gradually employed as workers as "permanent dependents" of their husbands. A few others came here to live with their relatives and gradually settled here.

In 1952 Rastriya Cha Mazdoor Congress (RCMC), the Congress sponsored labour union, was started in this tea plantation and consequently the Tea District Labour Association was dissolved in 1959. Since then recruitment of labourers in this plantation was made through the RCMC union. The union not only played an important role in the labour-management relations by mutualising tensions but also took an active role in labour recruitment. These new recruits were often the "bonafide dependents" of the workers of Chandmoni plantation. So the new recruits from outside were totally stopped after the establishment of trade unions in the garden.

Among the existing workers of this plantation 123 had come from various places like Bihar, Madhya Pradesh, Nepal and Bangladesh. Eighty of them belong to various Adivasi communities and 43 to non-Adivasis. This immigrant population either came to this garden themselves in search of jobs as workers or they were brought by some Sardars who were later recruited by the plantation authority as workers. Some of them who could be considered as "permanent dependents" of the workers were also recruited as labourers. A good number of them came from different gardens of Terai and Dooars or from the neighbouring regions. They were either recruited through the Sardars or directly by the plantation authority. Only a few workers of the plantation were recruited through some private agencies in Ranchi. There are 6 labourers who were recruited through this process of whom 4 are male and 2 are female. Among the other workers 105 males and 97 females were recruited through the Sardars. Twenty one male and 9 female workers were directly recruited by the plantation authority. Besides, there are recruitment of 120 male, 113 female and 36 child workers through the unions. This recruitment was made either to fill the vacant posts or to absorb the "bonafide dependents" of the workers in lieu of the deseased or retired relatives. Sometimes a few recruitments through the "paddy land demand" was also done.[17] In this garden so far 108 male, 75 female and 20 child workers were recruited in the vacant posts and a few newly created posts through the unions for filling up the "permanent dependent" as well as "bonafide dependent" vacancies. One males, 11 females and 5 children were recruited in the vacancies created through the "paddy land demand" by the union. Nineteen male, 27 female and 11 child workers were recruited in the vacant positions created by their deceased or retired relatives.

Nature of Women's Work in the Plantation

It is very significant that sometimes women workers outnumber men in the plantations. In regard to the various jobs of wage-earners on which women are employed it may be said that in a plantation there is no rigid classification of workers. The entire working force of the plantation is devided into two broad categories — garden labours and staff. The bulk of the working force constitutes the first category and those in the second are very few in number. All operations connected with plantation are allotted to the garden labourers. When a woman is appointed as a garden labourer, she may be required to attend any type of work that may be assigned to her by the management. Generally plantation operations on which women work are plucking, weeding, transplanting, etc. Adivasi women are never found to be appointed to posts relating to the managerial, executive or administrative work nor are they employed in the clerical or allied positions. Practically the women workers here have no promotion facilities. We shall later on discuss this problem in some details. In every stratum of the plantation hierarchy men have monopolised more responsible positions, which are often better paid.

Types of Work

In the Terai plantations tea bushes are allowed to grow a maximum height of three feet. In the natural process a tea bush can grow upto a maximum height of eighteen to twenty feet. But in a plantation tea bushes are kept to a stunted growth of about three feet as such a height gives the lagest number of plucking points. The other factor is that such a height is convenient for the men and women workers of the graden as plucking is done by hand. The plucked leaves are comprised of two leaves on either side and a bud in between.

The daily wage workers of the tea plantation perform all types of manual work such as plucking of leaves, weeding, hoeing, manuring, forking and cleaning and soil, pruning the tea bushes in winter, taking care of nursery bed of young tea plants and cleaning the tea stalks in the factory (Table 23). Most of the labourers employed for plucking (Patti-tepai) are women. The men workers also pluck leave occasionally. Then men workers are often engaged in hoeing (Thali-pharua), cleaning the ground around the bushes (Khulni), spraying of pesticides, and so on.

The period from May to November is generally regarded as the busy season in the tea plantation. July to September is the peak period of the plucking season and the workers; specially the women workers can earn entire wages from plucking over the required norm. December to March is the slack season in plantation. During this period the earning of the women workers as well as the average earning of the labour family remains generally lower. During the slack season in winter the volume of

Table 23

Sex-wise Classification of Plantation Work

	Operation in Garden and Factory	Period in Month	Sex of Workers
	Garden operations		
1.	Filling of vacancies of tea bushes	January - May	Men, Women
2.	Transplanting	January - March	Men, Women
3.	Manuring	February - May	Men, Women
4.	Tipping	March - April	Men, Women
5.	Plucking	March - December	Men, Women
6.	Spraying pesticide	April - September	Men
7.	Pruning	October - January	Men, Women
8.	Weeding	Throughout the year	Men, Women
9.	Hoeing	Throughout the year	Men, Women
	Factory operations		
10.	Machine operating	March - December	Men
11.	Withering	March - December	Men
12.	Rolling	March - December	Men
13.	Fermenting	March - December	Men
14.	Drying	March - December	Men
15.	Sorting	March - December	Men, Women
16.	Packing	March - December	Men

work as well as working hours reduces considerably. Women workers of the plantation remain busy at least for a large part of the year, while the men workers can enjoy leisure when work in the plantation is over. In some cases, the women workers in the plantation work even longer hours than the men. In the north Indian tea gardens, the work system for men is that of "task-work", which means that when the task for the day is done, the work is over. Normally four to five hours are needed to complete the work under the system. While women workers employed in plucking at "piece-rate" are to work for seven to eight hours in order to earn the minimum daily wage. The plucking season generally begins with the early rains in March and ends either in November or in early December. The plucking gives the highest yield during July to August when rainfall is heavy. The plucking of the early monsoon is supposed to produce the best quality of tea.

After the plucking is over the bushes are pruned. Such pruning is made from six inches to eighteen inches. The pruning can be divided into light, medium and deep on the basis of the height of the pruning. Pruning of tea bushes is a very important task in the garden. The yield of the season depends on how the bushes are pruned. So such pruning is done by the efficient men workers of the garden. Light and medium pruning (Kalam-kata) are only done by young and efficient women workers. But the deep pruning is only done by the efficient men workers as it requires both efficiency and physical strength. The men workers also perform other hard works such as deep-hoeing, digging and spraying of pesticide and weedicide. The work in which women are generally employed are plucking of leaf. They also do weeding, manuring, light hoeing (Thali-pharua), collecting the seeds of the shade trees, forking (Jilloni) and preparing nursery beds. In many works in the plantation the women workers are as efficient as the men workers, and it is believed that in some work such as plucking the women workers are more efficient than the men. In plucking the women workers score over the men workers both in efficiency and quality of leaves plucked. The men workers also pluck tea leaves, but it is generally found that the quality as well as quantity of leaves plucked are not as high as those of the women workers. There is a reason behind it. The plucking of good quality of tea leaves requires patience, and for this the women workers are more suitable than the men workers. Other factor may be that the men workers prefer the work which requires greater physical labour, such as hoeing, digging, etc. However, the women workers in the plantation are always given light work. During the peak season, i.e., from April to November they remain busy in plucking, and during the slack season they are employed in light and medium pruning, forking and wedding. Pruning in plantation can be considered as semi-skilled work. Only young and efficient women workers are allotted for pruning. However they are very few in number. In the factory of the tea plantation aged and weak women are employed in picking out the stalks (Chunsi) from the tea leaves. Sometimes the aged men and women workers are engaged in making nursery seed beds. The women and adolescent workers perform the same type of work. Children are generally given light agricultural work such as removing creepers and parasites from the tea bushes, light digging, collecting the seeds of shade trees, etc.

Generally a work in the plantation is done in groups. Under the supervision of Dafadars or Sardars the workers are divided into several groups. A group is consisted of about fifty workers either men or women. The Dafadars generally supervise the plucking of leaf in the plantation. The Sardars supervise the other work. The work is generally allotted in gangs or Patti. Some are allotted to plucking leaves while others to hoeing, etc.

The System of Work and Working Hours

The Plantation Labour Act, 1951 which applied to non-factory workers of plantation lays down the maximum weekly working hours for adults at 54 and for adolescent and children at 40. It also prescribes that after five hours of work a worker must be allowed to have an interval for rest of at least half an hour. The period of work of an adult worker inclusive of intervals for rest and the time spent for waiting for work on any one day shall not be spread over more than 12 hours.

According to a review of the working of the Plantation Labour Act for the year 1957, normal weekly hours of work were 24 in Bihar, ranged between 39 and 51 in Uttar Pradesh and between 37 and 47 in West Bengal.[18] The Act provides for a day of rest in every period of seven days, and for the payment for work done on a day of rest. The Act also provides for grant of leave with wages at the rate of one day for every twenty days of work for adults. For adolescent and children the rate is one day for every fifteen working days. Accumulation of leave is allowed up to a maximum of 30 days. In some cases, women workers work even longer hours than the men.

In tea plantation a worker is allotted to a certain piece of work which he or she has to complete within a given period of time. This is known as Thika. The Thika tasks are fixed either in terms of bushes or Dangs or Nals. A Nal or Dang is an area of 12 square feet and roughly 3000 Nals comprise an acre. The tasks assigned to women and children for their Hazira are proportionately less than the men. The amount of each of the tasks which the workers perform are discussed here. Approximately 8 to 16 Nals of land is given to a man worker for deep hoeing in a day. A man is required to complete light hoeing in about 40 to 48 Nals of land in a day. The deep pruning operation is to be done in 60 to 72 bushes in a day by a man worker; he has to perform light pruning in about 60 to 180 bushes in a day whereas he can perform forking and weeding of 160 to 240 bushes within the same time. However, a woman worker has to do light pruning in about 60 to 100 bushes or forking and weeding in about 160 to 200 bushes in a day. In the Thika in which a woman worker is engaged in plucking has to pluck a fixed amount of tea leaves. In Chandmoni Tea Estate the amount of leaves to be plucked by a labourer vary from 15 to 22 kilograms per day. The minimum fixed quantity of leaf plucking varies from season to season. The manager and the Bagan-babu decide the minimum quantity of leaves to be plucked. The men and women workers have no say in this matter. They pluck more and can earn more by over plucking. In the Thika where other types of work are to be done a labourer works on a specific number of tea bushes in the garden as mentioned earlier or on a specific area of the tea estate. After completion she is paid a wage for her tasks or Thika which is known as Haxri. If a worker is engaged in plucking he or she will get an incentive of 10 paise for every kilogram of leaves plucked in excess of Thika of a fixed amount of leaves which varies from 15 to 22 kilograms in a day from season to season. Over plucking is commonly known as Dubly. During pruning, every adult and efficient worker is allotted a specific number of tea bushes which he or she has to prune. In the slack season some of the workers are engaged in miscellaneous work which cannot easily be measured on a piece rate basis. Such works are repair of roads and bridges, erecting fences, etc. for which they are paid on time basis. These works are generally done by men workers and they are given basic wages for work of 5 to 6 hours. Again, early in the plucking season there will not be sufficient flush on the tea bushes to enable the pluckers to earn their basic wages if the plucking like Chhatni-patti or Ticca is adopted. In the Ticca plucking early in the season there may be a danger if the plucking of leaf is done indiscriminately, because it may spoil the flushing surface of the tea bushes. Like in all other tea plantations the workers of the Chandmoni Tea Estate also get payment on the time basis for the first few rounds of plucking usually called tipping. The time required to spend on his work is generally 6 to 7 hours a day. Similarly towards the end of the flushing season also plucking on time basis is followed. Other workers engaged in the plantation are herdsmen, water-carrier (Paniwalla), etc. All of them are men workers.

The Wages of the Women Workers

The daily wage workers are paid on the basis of time as well as piece rate work. Normally they are to work eight hours in a day and six days in a week. A worker is paid for his or her minimum daily wages (Hazri) for this work. He or she is given a specific amount of work which he or she has to complete during the working hours.

Wages in the plantation industry varied from place to place according to the employment, market condition and living standard in the areas where the plantations were located. It also varied on the basis of supply of labour in tea plantations. In North India average daily earnings of women and men unskilled labours differed by only some 5 to 15 per cent, and the differences in wage rates for similar work was sometimes even smaller. In South Indian plantations, sex differentials in wages were considerably larger.[19] Plantations were included in the Scheduled Employment under the Minimum Wage Act, 1948. The act required the State Government to fix the minimum rates of wages payable to employees working in Scheduled Employments. Where minimum rates of wages had been fixed and notified, the State Government had to review these rates at least once in five years, and the employer was bound by law to pay every employee engaged in Scheduled Employment under him wages at a rate not less than the minimum rates of wages fixed for a particular class of employees.[20] The payment of Wage Act of 1936 made it compulsory for the employer to pay the agreed minimum wage. The 15th session of the Indian Labour Conference held in July, 1957 agreed that the workers in all major industries should not only have a guaranteed minimum wage but a need-based minimum wage. The tea plantation wage board was appointed in December, 1960.

In plantations in the Terai region including Chandmoni Tea Estate the first interim increment of wage was introduced among the daily-rated workers in 1962. The recommendations of the Central Wage Board were declared on 1st April, 1966. In Terai plantations twice there was an interim wage increment of 8 paise and 6 paise for both men and women workers. The increment was same in case of plantations of Dooars. Thus just before the final recommendations, the wages of the tea plantation workers in Terai stood at Rs. 1.95 for men, Rs. 1.81 for women and Rs. 1.07 for children whereas in Dooars it stood at Rs. 1.98 for men, Rs. 1.84 for women and Rs. 1.07 for children. In the plantations which are less than 500 acres in size workers get wage 3 paise less than the normal wages. The board recommended that wages for men, women and children be increased by 13 paise, 10 paise and 7 paise respectively from January, 1966, and a further increase of 2 paise for men and women and 1 paise for children from 1st April, 1966. In this garden according to the Terai Planters Negotiation Act, August, 1966 wages increased by 12 paise for men, 9 paise for women and 6 paise for children. The difference between the wages of men and women workers increased from 14 paise to 17 paise. Thus the new wage for the workers was the "need-based wage" and the standard formula for fixing such need-based minimum wage was to consider 3 units of consumption for every adult man worker.[21]

From 1966 to 1975 wages gradually increased either through the recommendations of bipartite meetings or through the demand of the trade union of the plantation workers. In plantations of the Terai region as well as in Chandmoni Tea Estate from 2nd September, 1969 to 31st March, 1970 the wages were Rs. 2.39 for men, Rs. 2.22 for women and Rs. 1.29 for children. From 1st April, 1970 to 30th June, 1971 it was raised to Rs. 2.48 for men, Rs. 2.31 for women, Rs. 1.33 for children and from 1st July, 1971 to 31st May, 1972 the wage was raised to Rs. 2.71 for men, Rs. 2.54 for women and Rs. 1.45 for children. From 1st June, 1972 to 30th June, 1973 the wage was raised to Rs. 2.94 for men, Rs. 2.77 for women and Rs. 1.56 for children. The wage for adolescent was similar to that of women. The wages of the plantation workers in Dooars then stood at Rs. 3.00 for men, Rs. 2.83 for women and Rs. 1.50 for children. In April 1973, the Second Minimum Wage Fixation Committee for Tea Plantations was appointed by the State Government. This committee finalised the minimum wages in July, 1977.

The wages in plantations were graduallay enhanced and the wage differentiation between men and women workers continued. In between the period July, 1973 and June, 1977 there was an increase of 15 paise for adult men and women workers and 7 paise for children. There was again an increase of 25 paise for the adult workers and 12 paise for children during the period from July, 1974 to June, 1975. The wage was then Rs. 3.34 for men, Rs. 2.77 for women and Rs. 1.76 for children. Again there was an interim increase of 45 paise during the period between July, 1975 and March, 1976. In between the period from April, 1976 to June, 1977 there was again an increase of 45 paise. Then the wage reached to Rs. 4.24 for men, Rs. 4.07 for women and Rs. 2.21 for children workers. In the meantime the second Minimum Wage Fixation Committee finalised the minimum wages on 24 July, 1977. In between July, 1977 and June, 1978 there was again an increase of Rs. 1.00. The wage for men was Rs. 5.24, for women Rs. 5.07 and for children Rs. 2.73. Between July, 1978 and June, 1979 there was again an increase of interim wages of Rs. 1.00. The Dubly was then enhanced from 8 paise to 10 paise per kilogram for extra leaf plucking.

The wage difference between men and women workers was abolished in December, 1976. But many of the employers in Terai and Dooars refused to pay equal wages even after the equal wage for equal work Act was passed. In Chandmoni Tea Estate it was not implemented upto July, 1979. We have seen that since the beginning of the plantation industry there was wage difference between men and women workers. This difference had gradually been reduced during the post-Independence period mainly through implementing the Minimum Wage Act.

The Indian Tea Planters' Association (ITPA) is in favour of maintaining the wage difference between men and women workers in plantation. They think it necessary because the work-load for women workers is always less than that of men. The Thika assigned to women workers is always lesser than that of men workers. The ITPA thinks that if workers are given equal wages irrespective of sex and at the same time different workloads are allotted to them, it will be a discrimination against men.[22] However, this discrimination is still maintained in the plantations of the Terai and Dooars region. In Chandmoni Tea Estate, in the Thika in plucking tea leaves for men was 25 kilograms and for women workers it was 22 kilograms in a day during the peak season of 1979.

The Dearness Allowance forms a part of the revised wages of the plantation workers fixed under the Minimum Wage Act. Besides, a plantation worker gets ration at concessional rates. Annually a worker receives 5 quintals of fire wood whereas a sub-staff gets 6 quintals. Some protective uniforms which are essential for working in the plantation are also supplied free to the workers. Apron and umbrella are such articles. Each worker receives from the authority a blanket once in every two years free of cost.

Housing and Creche Facilities

Earlier the labourers were recruited from the remote villages of Bihar and Madhya Pradesh, and they were brought along with their families. This provided the owners not only with a steady source of supply of labour but also they could exercise a close control over the workers.

In the tea plantation of Dooars, the houses are built in 'barrack lines' scattered over the gardens. In the lines each house has usually its own separate compound, though in many cases the houses are built quite close to each other in rows. The houses in the tea plantations of the Terai region are similar to those of

Dooars. In Darjeeling houses are built clustered on terraces. In tea gardens all the houses are rarely Pucca made of brick walls, cement floors and tin, tiled or asbestos roofs. A large proportion of them yet remain thatched hovels with mud or bamboo walls though as per the terms of Plantation Act, 1951 these should have been made Pucca. In Chandmoni Tea Estate there are both Kachha and Pucca houses. Almost all the houses have a small fenced compound which is used as a kitchen garden for growing vegetables, maize, etc. Those who possess cattle build cattle shed near the house. Usually the Kachha houses are repaired once in two years. Materials such as bamboo and straw are supplied by the owner of the garden.

In every plantation where fifty or more women workers are employed the employer is required to provide and maintain a creche for the children who are below the age of six years. In Chandmoni Tea Estate there is a creche with two female attendants who generally look after the children of the workers. On demand of the workers the management has arranged for the free supply of milk and Muri to the children. But most of the workers do not like to keep their children in the creche. They say, "The atmosphere is very bad and food, milk, water, etc. are not properly supplied by the management".

Health and Sanitation Facilities

The Plantation Labour Act, 1951 has a provision for adequate supply of drinking water in the plantation particularly at the work sites, and also for the proper storage of water and cleanliness of well or reservoir constructed within the plantation. This Act also provides for sanitary latrine in every plantation on the basis of one latrine for every fifty acres of the area under cultivation. However, no such latrine has yet been constructed for the workers of the Chandmoni Tea Estate. For drinking water seven wells have been constructed by the management so that at least one well is allotted to each residential line. As these wells are not sufficient for the plantation population some of the households have dug their own Kachha well. Obviously these wells and the other poorly maintained Pucca wells are a source of water-born diseases.

Health has two aspects, incidence of diseases and measures

to mitigate such incidence. The first is reflected in the death rate and the second in medical facilities. The common diseases in the Chandmoni Tea Estate are cholera, malarial fever, diarrhoea, tuberculosis, hookworm, respiratory diseases, leprosy, gastro-enteritis and diseases relating to maternity cases. Among these, tuberculosis, anaemia, gastro-enteritis and diarrhoea cause death to a good number of individuals. Considerable number of death occurs due to 'other diseases' also.

Formerly in Chandmoni Tea Estate there was a hospital. Recently due to lack of facilities it has been reduced to a dispensary. The medical staff of the plantation consists of a doctor, a compounder, a dresser-cum-health assistant and a woman attendant. There is no qualified nurse or midwife. Due to the lack of proper management and finance the hospital cannot provide services to the plantation workers. Scarcity of medicines has become a common feature of the "health facilities" available to the workers.

The Plantation Labour Act, 1951 provides that every worker is entitled to enjoy a medical leave for a period of 14 days in a year at the rate of two third of his or her daily minimum wages.

The rules regarding maternity provide that every woman employed in a plantation is entitled to enjoy a maternity leave with full-pay for a period of six weeks immediately proceeding the expected day of her delivery and for a period of six weeks immediately following the day of her delivery. Ration at concessional rates is also available during this period. In case a woman dies within six weeks of the delivery, the maternity wages are then given to the person who undertakes the care of the child.

Educational Facilities

The Plantation Labour Act, 1951 provides that every employer should, if the number of workers' children between the age of 6 and 12 in plantation exceed 25, provide and maintain a primary school for the primary education of children. In Chandmoni Tea Estate there is also a primary school but a considerable number of the students are outsiders. Out of a total of 300 students only 73 boys and 29 girls are the children of the workers and rest are the outsiders.

Holidays and Recreational Facilities

At present the tea plantation workers enjoy paid holidays on the Independence Day, Republic Day and May Day. In addition, there are four paid festival holidays of which two days are for Durga Puja, one day each for Diwali and Holi.

The rules provide that every employer should provide and maintain recreation centre or centres for workers with provision for a radio set and indoor games suitable for adult and child workers, and where adequate flat open space is available within a reasonable distance, a playground for adult and child workers with necessary sports equipments for outdoor games. In Chandmoni Tea Estate the workers are provided with football, volleyball, and a playground by the plantation authority. However, recreational facilities for women are thought not necessary. There is no club either for men or women workers. The women have no roles in creativity and aesthetic. During leisure they only gossip and sometimes they visit their relatives in the other residential lines of the tea estate.

ATTITUDES AND COMMITMENT

Attitude Towards Plantation Work

An analysis of the plantation women workers' attitude towards their work and objective situation will remain incomplete unless the real reasons of taking up wage work in the tea plantation are understood properly. The women workers have come out of their home to work as wage earners. Their job motives are obviously different from those of the middle class educated working women. Middle class working women are induced both by economic necessity of the family as well as by the emerging emancipatory condition. In most cases these two motives co-exist side by side. The reasons for taking up employment by middle class working women are : (i) family oriented economic reasons, (ii) striving towards individual self-fulfilment and emancipation, and (iii) desire to use one's leisure time. It is seen that these motivations do not exclude one another but are interrelated. The work motives of the educated middle class women are not primarily oriented towards the need of the family but they are striving more towards individual self-fulfilment and self-realisation. Sometimes there is a genuine emancipatory tendency behind their work.

It is found that the earnings of the middle class educated working wives are often regarded as a subsidiary, as a help to buy "extras". They use the work for a secondary source of income. Basically such income is utilised for home decoration or to buy consumers goods and clothing, to enjoy holidays and to avoid unnecessary loneliness. In case of the backward class plantation women workers' earnings are considered as essential contribution to support their families. However, in both the cases money is undoubtedly the largest incentive for the married women to go out to work. Work in the plantation has increasingly been normal and essential component of a woman's daily life. It is a common fact that all the women workers have taken up employment out of economic consideration and not to fulfil their own individual needs. However, I am trying to explore here five broad aspects of the employment situation of plantation women; their attitude towards work, attitude towards the company as the employer, attitude towards pay and other facilities, attitude towards the management and lastly attitude towards their immediate supervisor.

Women workers' attitude towards work is directly related to their position in the life cycle. Womens' participation in the labour force is responsive to the major life cycle events as education, marriage, divorce, child bearing and geographical mobility. Thus variations in attitude are assumed to depend primarily on difference in age, marital status and presence or absence of dependent relatives. But among the plantation women workers there is little variation of opinion. In most cases the backward class uneducated plantation women workers have largely gone into plantation work as it requires little skill and carry small responsibility. To them plantation work is 'just' a job like any other for fulfilment of their economic needs. In case of plantation system women as compared to men, display no consistently attenuated level of occupational aspirations. Plantation women are not characterised by a qualitatively different orientation towards work from that exhibited by their male counterpart. There is no documentation of differing expectations and aspirations at the point of entry into the labour market though there is a motivational difference.

From the opinion of the plantation women workers it is found that due to some reasons they prefer plantation work and they do not like to move to any other job. One of the reasons is that the plantation provides them security of job. All members of the family are provided with jobs by the plantation authority. Moreover, as they have come from an agricultural society they can easily adapt themselves to plantation work which is somewhat akin to agricultural work. Other reason is that as the plantation authority provides them residential accommodation women can work in plantation without seriously disturbing their family duties. Majority of the women workers here are of the opinion that women's job and their family duties harmoniously complement each other. About 89.1 per cent of the women workers stated that plantation work and work at home are of equal importance to them. The rest of the women workers gave more weightage to household duties. The principle of utilising every ablebodied person of the workers' family as labourer in the plantation, residence within the plantation and nature of work have attracted women, to a large extent, to seek employment in this industry. In Chandmoni Tea Estate out of 221 women workers 14 (6.33 per cent) are unmarried who earn only to support themselves and their parents, 188 (85.06 per cent) women workers are married who are working as primary bread winners to support their families, only 12 (5.42 per cent) widow women workers earn to support their children and themselves, and 7 (3.16 per cent) women are working because their husbands are either invalid or suffering from diseases like leprosy and tuberculosis.

The women workers are significantly more satisfied with their wages than the men workers. However, promotion opportunities, though very limited, are only open to the men workers of the plantation. While the women workers, inspite of being recognised as committed workers, as mentioned by the management, cannot move up in the job hierarchy. The men workers, although only few, can move up to occupy positions of Sardar, Dafadar, Boidar, Chaprasi and Munshi. These higher positions are provided with slightly higher wages than those of the ordinary labourers. These positions also enjoy some power and privileges. But the women workers never grumble for such discrimination. Their awareness is not upto that limit. Their job satisfaction is mainly due to certain facilities given to them. They quite often mention that they get free-quarter, fire-wood, ration at subsidy rate, cultivable land, bonus and other facilities from the plantation authority without any trouble. Many of these facilities are not provided by other industries to their workers. There is no vertical mobility in the occupational hierarchy but the women workers do not seem to have any frustration simply because their expectation out of the employment is limited. Their socialization process also helps them to accept the plantation occupation as their family occupation and has made them unconcerned about their low position in the industry. Their attitude seems not susceptible to change as they have less education and less outer influence.

The plantation women workers were also asked how the relatives, family, friends and other fellow workers evaluated their occupation. Most of them felt that their families, relatives, friends and other co-workers evaluated their occupation positively. In their attitude towards the Chandmoni Tea Estate as the employer, all the women workers were remarkably alike. When they were asked to name the best things about working for the Chandmoni Tea Estate, the three most frequently mentioned items were the security of employment, the good physical working conditions, the fringe benefits such as maternity benefits, sick pay, bonus, provident fund, etc. Only 25 (11.31 per cent) women out of 221 women workers said that the plantation work was an interesting job. Out of 221 women workers 213 (96.38 per cent) said that they wished to stay in this tea estate until their retirement. They never thought of leaving. There was little variation in the reasons for wanting to stay. Two third of the women workers mentioned the attraction of fringe benefits and the employment security provided by the employer of the tea estate.

The low level of education is positively related to the low occupational aspirations of the plantation workers. The level of education in plantation, specially among the women is very low. Out of 47 literate women 38 (3.04 per cent) have primary education and 9 (0.72 per cent) have secondary education. It is interesting that the plantation women workers do not have any aspirations for better employment and better standard of living. Employment being family based to some extent automatically restricts the choice of occupation. However, a direct comparison of aspiration of men and women workers is somewhat difficult as their jobs in the plantation are not always the same. Moreover men workers' jobs are more open than those of the women workers. In general both men and women have low aspiration which is also due to their ethno-cultural background. It is significant to note that in general all the women workers in the plantation expect their sons and daughters to follow their parents' occupation. However, a few men workers show fairly high aspiration for their son's educational and occupational future. A few cases of aspiration regarding the future of their sons and daughters of both men and women workers will make the statement clear. Gondra Munda (29) is a Boidar (attendance keeper) of Chandmoni who has education upto class X standard. He belongs to the Saonsar religion. He possesses a high aspiration about the future of his sons. Gondra said, "My father did not provide me opportunity for higher education, but I shall provide my sons. My three sons are studying in St. Mary's Convent School, Siliguri. I spend about Rs. 150 per month for their education. I shall give them enough opportunity for higher education so that they can get clerical or other jobs elsewhere". Although he does not have a daughter he advocates female education. His wife Gita Munda (26) is a worker in Chandmoni who has no formal education. Gita has expressed that she has no idea of the future of her sons, education and employment. All these depend on her husband. But she likes that her sons should accept occupation in the tea plantation. Ramjatan Naik (27) is a Ghasi who works in Chandmoni as a Boidar. He follows the Saonsar religion. Ramjatan has read upto class X standard. He has a training from the Workers' Education Centre, Siliguri. He spends about Rs. 60 per month for education of his two sons two are studying in the Prince Nursery School, Siliguri. Ramjatan says that without education it is very difficult to get any job outside. Although occupation in the plantation is not bad, now-a-days to get a good job education is essential. He also possesses a positive attitude regarding female education. Ramjatan's wife Butain Naik (24) is an illiterate who works in Chandmoni. Butain says that as she does not have education she does not have aspiration for better jobs. According to her it is essential to have education for getting better employment. Although she does not possess much aspiration about her sons' education and occupation she says that they should get education for better employment in tea plantation. Illias Soren (44) and his wife Carmela Soren (40) hail from Keria community who are Christians. Illias is educated upto class VII and works as a health assistant. Carmela has read upto class V and works in the same plantation. They have two daughters and a son. Both of them have a high aspiration regarding their son's and daughters' education and employment. The son has appeared in ICSC examination from St. Mary's Boarding School, Nagrakata and a daughter is studying in St. Mary's School, Siliguri. Their another daughter has read upto class VI in the St. Peter School, Gayaganga and is now working in Chandmoni. They spend about Rs. 150 per month for their education and put equal importance for male and female education. They emphasize the importance of female education. According to them education improves respect and economic condition of the family and it also provides better employment outside the tea plantation. Karlus Oraon (45), a Chaprasi is a Christian. Benidicts Oraon (36) is his wife who also works in Chandmoni. Both of them have no formal education. They have four daughters and one son. Both of them have a high aspirtation about education and employment of their son. But they are indifferent in respect of their daughters' education and employment. Their daughters are not enrolled in any school. The eldest daughter is working in Chandmoni Tea Estate. Their son is studying in St. Peter School, Gayaganga and stays in the school hostel. They spend Rs. 100 per month for their son's education on the hope that he will get a better job in the tea plantation or outside. But they think that their daughters should take up plantation job. Emilleous Kalko (31) and his wife Kelmensia Khalko (27) belong to the Oraon community who are Christians. Emilleous and Kelmensis are educated upto class X and VIII respectively. Immilleous works in water supply department in the Military Engineering Services (MES) at Bagdogra and gets Rs. 300 per month. But Kelmensia is a worker in Chandmoni. They live within Chandmoni Tea Estate. They have a son and a daughter. Their son is studying in St. Peter School, Gayaganga and stays in the hostel. They wish that their son and daughter should be given education equally which would enable them to take up jobs outside the plantation. Both of them do not prefer plantation work. Kelmensia says that she will leave the plantation if she gets an employment elsewhere.

There are differences at the aspiration level between the Adivasi workers and non-Adivasi workers belonging particularly to the Nepalis. It is noticed that the caste workers aspire more than those belonging to the Adivasis in respect of their own future as well as education and employment of their sons. But they are not keen about women's education. Two cases of Nepali workers are given below : Ranbahadur Pradhan (55) is a Chowkidar who has no formal education. His wife Bishnumaya Pradhan (55) was a worker in Chandmoni, but she left the job in 1976 due to illness. They have three sons and a daughter. Both of them have high ambition for their sons. Their one son is a matriculate who works in the Indian Army. Other two sons are studying in the high school. Their only daughter has read upto class III. They do not like to employ their daughter in the plantation and want that the sons should do white-collar jobs. Dilbahadur Chhetri (40) is also a Chowkidar in Chandmoni and his wife Umadevi Chhetri (32) is also a worker there. Although they do not have any formal education they aspire high for their sons' education and employment. Four sons and two daughters are studying in School in Siliguri. Both of them do not like that their sons and daughters should work in the tea plantation. They aspire for better employment and white-collar jobs for their sons. But they do not have any high hope for their daughters' future. They have a plan that after retirement they would go back to their native village in Bhojpur, Nepal.

In this tea estate most of the women workers are illiterate as I have mentioned earlier, and are unskilled labourers and their participation in the working class movement is very slowly emerging. Active participation against management is very poorly presented by the women workers. All the employees have direct access to the management which helps to mitigate their grievances to some extent. They never criticize management spontaneously. The plantation authority and the supervisors are also more satisfied with the work participation of women workers than that of the men workers. And when we turn to examine attitudes to supervisors we find no difference of opinion between women workers. In case of the plantation work Sardar, Dafadar, Chaprasi, Munsi and Bagan-babus are the first line supervisors although in some cases it is the Manager himself looks after the work. They were asked, "Would you say you get on with your immediate supervisors very well"? all of them answered, "Generally our supervisors do not behave badly. Only when we neglect our work or cannot perform any work properly the supervisors behave rudely". A woman worker judges her work relations in terms of the rewards that occur from the work and considers the employment as obviously stable and permanent. This naturally makes her to ignore the occasional rebukes and reprimands from the supervisors.

Women Workers' Commitment to Plantation Work

The concept of commitment not only involves the performance of the workers but also the acceptance of the relevant norms of the industrial ways of life by them and orientation of their behaviour accordingly. The commitment of the workers to the industry can be explained in the sense of accepting discipline, learning new skills, producing efficiently and fighting for their rights as workers through the trade union. The commitment also implies the acceptance of new residential patterns, system of hierarchy and social goals, in addition to the system of factory production which involves responding to the rhythm and speed of the machine and the authority structure of the industry. The committed worker is one who has internalized these values and actualised them in his behaviour. He is one who has completely snapped his links with the village and land and has become an urban industrial man. Commitment also implies that labour is willing to shift from agriculture to industry. His wife also centers the labour market and he is conscious of his rights as a worker because industrial employment is his only source of security.[23] Scholars have used widely different measures and criteria of commitment. Some of these are attitude to employer and organization, stability of work force, availability of workers when needed. Sharma finds that social differences also influence the degree of commitment. According to him traditional Indian culture does not present any serious obstacles to the process of commitment.[24] Morris and Thorner have collected evidences leading to the conclusion that in most cases where workers are apparently uncommitted to their jobs, are due to the policies of recruitment and tenure adopted by the employers.[25] Morris has rightly argued that if absenteeism is to be taken as a criterion of lack of commitment, it will have to be defined as wilful non-attendance at work. He finds that industrial labour force has not been particularly unstable. The quantity of labour and the degree of commitment to industry are more a result of managerial policies and market forces than of the psychology of workers or their involvement in the traditional social structure of caste, kinship and village.[26]

A group of scholar has postulated the "logic of industrialism" and has argued that the essentially non-industrial characteristics of a society like India (e.g., relatively closed system of stratification, emphasis on primary group loyalty, religious values discouraging hard work and innovativeness, etc.) has obstructed workers' acceptance of the discipline and rigor of industrial activities.[27] This thesis has drawn attention of several sociologists to study Indian Industrial workers' commitment in the context of their social and cultural life. However, there are several dimensions of commitment such as psychological, social and economic. These dimensions should be studied in the context of industrial situations : recruitment and selection of workers, work place, work situation and conditions of employment, extra-industrial ways of life, etc. The workers come with different social backgrounds which also play a significant part in the process of commitment.

The plantation workers hail mostly from agricultural background and the industry itself is agro-based. The field operations of tea plantations are comparable to that of modern agriculture. So the plantation workers do not feel strangers to the new working environment and hence they could easily adjust themselves in this agro-industry. This also positively affect the commitment of both the men and women workers.

We have seen earlier that the recruitment policy in tea plantation was different from those of other industries. Here labourers were recruited from distant places who were given accommodation within the plantation. The recruitment was family as well as kinship based and the workers lived within the plantation close to each other. In many cases the management also provides small plots of agricultural land to most of the families. The management policies have motivated the workers to cut-off social relations to large extent from their native villages and land. Although during the earlier phase of recruitment immigrant workers had a great inclination to continue social relation with their homeland, but the first and second generations of the immigrants had used themselves to live within the plantation enviornment. The present generations of the immigrant labourers have to a large extent discontinued socia' relations with their homeland. In most of the cases the pres nt plantation workers are members of the second or third generation of the original migrants who had left their villages. They have adopted this occupation as their family occupation and both men, women and children of their families have joined in it. Such a situation also provides the workers to develop a high degree of commitment to their work. They are very much conscious of their work because they know that employment is their only source of income. They form an isolated society in the plantation environment which is completely separated from the neighbouring society. In most cases their social roots are well established in the plantation. Thus the plantation workers have become more committed than the workers of other industries. Workers were also recruited by the employer through the old workers of the plantation. In these informal process of selection friendship, kinship, ethnic background and village ties play an important role. This has some impact over the commitment of workers. The plantation workers' commitment is a life-long commitment and their loyalty is valued more than their efficiency.

A planter prefers to employ women for the working force as he thinks that women are more committed workers than their male counterpart. The planters make their work force committed by providing them with some apparenty attractive social and economic benefits. In every plantation there are standardized working hours and a rest day in a week. The employer provides housing and other welfare facilities, such as, free quarter, free fuel and fire-wood, free health services, free grazing land, cultivable land, maternity benefits, bonus, etc. which have perhaps made the conditions of employment more favourable to the plantation workers. As the workers live within the plantation obviously they have little difficulty in meeting the twin demands of society and plantation. Work in the plantation provides economic stability and security to the workers. Workers work in a world of kinsmen, neighbours and friends. It appears that their social life outside the work and their work within the plantation is an integral part of the same world rather than separate spheres of activity. All these facilities are not generally available in industries other than those of tea plantations. These have some positive effects upon the commitment of the labourers. Thus the plantation has become fully integrated into the life of the various Adivasi and caste people. The plantation workers are well disciplined and they are always under some routine. This may also be judged in the light of labour commitment. Lambert has shown that some sections of the Indian working force are "over-committed" in the sense that they wanted to stick to their employer without caring much of their prospects.[28] In that sense plantation workers are "over-committed" specially the women workers. Though in plantation, specially among the women workers, the upward mobility in the job is very much restricted but the job experience here determines the degree of commitment of women workers. Form is of the opinion that as the industrial workers move up in the occupational hierarchy, their commitment to industrial work increases.[29] But this does not apply to plantation. The plantation workers specially the women workers are committed workers though they do not move up in the occupational hierarchy.

The nature of the plantation system and its working population show a sharp difference from those of other industries. However, the nature of commitment of workers of plantation cannot be compared with that of the other industrial workers. We shall look at the commitment from a comparative perspective of men and women workers of plantation. Commitment of a worker is studied here by turnover and absenteeism. As in plantation there is a scope for earning extra wages from leaf plucking it is considered as a measure of commitment.

High turnover and absenteeism indicate an uncommitted work force. Generally turnover figures include everyone who leaves factory irrespective of why he leaves or what he does after leaving. Malhotra says that it is not correct to infer lack of commitment from 'turnover' unless it can be shown that a significant number of workers leave factory employment of their own volition and do not take up employment.[30] The turnover figure was very high in the plantation industry during the British period as labourers frequently ran away from plantations and the enticement of labourer was also very high. Since 1930's turnover had come down gradually. In general turnover was limited in the plantation industry due to three reasons : (a) until several decades ago labourers were restrained from leaving one garden for another until their period of indenture was over, (b) lack of opportunities in the rural matrix where the plantations were situated, and (c) there was positive effort on the part of plantation owners to keep their labour force as little unpolluted as possible from outside influence. This caused the gradual development of 'island society' in the plantation. In recent years turnover in plantation is not a problem at all as it has come down to a lowest level. It is significant to note that turnover of women workers is comparatively lower than that of men workers. In Chandmoni Tea Estate the total turnover of men and women workers was 0.57 per cent, 0.97 per cent, 0.78 per cent, 0.96 per cent and 0.19 per cent in 1977, 1978, 1979, 1980 and 1981 respectively. The women workers' turnover figure was nil in 1977 and 1981 while it was 0.38 per cent, 0.39 per cent and 0.38 per cent in 1978, 1979 and 1980 respectively. These figures were comparatively lower than those of the men workers (Table 24). It is revealed from the turnover figures of men and women workers that the latter are more committed to the plantation work than the former.

Table 24

Turnover of Men and Women Workers in Chandmoni

Year	Total Number of Workers	Workers Turnover Men %	Workers Turnover Women %	Total %
1977	520	3 (0.57)	-	3 (0.57)
1978	515	3 (0.58)	2 (0.38)	5 (0.97)
1979	511	2 (0.39)	2 (0.39)	4 (0.78)
1980	520	3 (0.57)	2 (0.38)	5 (0.96)
1981	520	1 (0.19)	-	1 (0.19)

In tea plantations daily wage workers got Rs. 6.24 per day in 1980. Although the wages were enhanced to Rs. 8.12 in July, 1979, the workers of Chandmoni were not given the enhanced amount even in 1980. Along with the daily wages the plantation workers, who can pluck more than the amount fixed (Thika) by the management, can earn extra wages. This extra wage earning is only possible in the operation of leaf plucking. A certain amount of skill is necessary in the operation of tea leaf plucking. Obviously sincerity of the worker to this operation is an important factor. It is observed that some workers pluck less than the amount fixed in the Thika, some others can just complete the Thika, while some others can pluck more than the Thika. This shows that some workers are less committed, while some other are more committed. In the study of commitment of plantation workers extra wage earning from leaf plucking is one of the important indicators of commitment. We are interested here to know the differences at the level of commitment between men and women workers in the operation of leaf plucking. Leaf plucking is the most important operation because it is done during the period from March to December. Out data show that women workers are more committed than the men workers in Chandmoni. In 1980, 232 Women workers were engaged in the operation of leaf plucking who had earned extra wages of Rs. 39.71 per head on an average for plucking of tea leaf more than the amount fixed in the Thika. In that year the Thika of leaf plucking was 22 kg. per worker and the leaf wage was fixed at 10 paise per extra kg. Whereas in the same year 189 men workers were engaged in this operation and they had earned Rs. 25.33 per head on an average. In general it can be said that women workers are more committed to their work than the men workers of Chandmoni. From the data it is also seen that women workers of Goswami, Mahali, Bhokta, Lohar and Bihari communities had earned less extra wages than their men workers from the extra leaf plucking. Reasons behind the less commitment of these women were their old age, more number of children and breast-feeding baby and inefficiency (Table 25). Of the two largest Adivasi communities the Munda women appear to be more committed than the Oraon women in so far the leaf plucking is concerned.

Absenteeism is another indicator of commitment. It refers to the tendency on the part of a worker to abstain from his or her scheduled work. Absenteeism can be studied in many ways because the reasons for such absence vary from industry to industry. However if absenteeism is to be taken as a criterion of lack of commitment it will have to be clearly defined as wilful non-attendance of work. A number of work-related factors are responsible for absenteeism. Sinha has grouped such factors under the following heads: (a) in-plant causes, (b) personal causes, and

Table 25

Extra Wages Earned by the Daily Wage-Workers Engaged in Leaf Plucking in 1980

Adivasi and Caste	Number of Workers	Total Extra Wages Earned (in Rs.)	Average Extra Wages per Man Worker (in Rs.)	Number of Workers	Total Extra Wages Earned (in Rs.)	Average Extra Wages per Woman Worker (in Rs.)
Adivasi						
Oraon	69	1843.56	26.71	84	2855.78	34.00
Munda	36	1035.15	28.75	50	3285.23	65.70
Kheria	4	72.34	18.08	5	242.11	48.42
Meher	2	11.44	5.72	–	–	–
Baraik	11	147.14	13.37	11	323.20	29.38
Goswami	2	14.43	7.21	4	15.37	3.84
Saosi	5	172.65	34.53	4	146.76	36.69
Bairagi	1	1.82	1.82	2	106.10	53.05
Goala	3	40.75	13.58	2	66.69	33.34
Malpahari	7	77.19	11.03	11	336.81	30.62
Mahali	6	247.28	41.21	7	38.46	5.49
Bhokta	1	118.82	118.82	3	71.85	23.95
Korowa	5	25.17	5.03	6	170.65	28.44

Contd...

Adivasi and Caste	Number of Workers	Total Extra Wages Earned (in Rs.)	Average Extra Wages per Man Worker (in Rs.)	Number of Workers	Total Extra Wages Earned (in Rs.)	Average Extra Wages per Woman Worker (in Rs.)
Lohar	5	250.11	50.02	6	162.35	27.05
Turi	2	72.22	36.11	2	127.42	63.71
Ore	1	0.52	.52	1	68.12	68.12
Ghasi	14	336.31	24.02	15	385.74	25.72
Toutia	–	–	–	–	–	–
Bhuiyan	–	–	–	–	–	–
Caste						
Bengali	–	–	–	–	–	–
Bihari	5	117.93	23.58	2	44.11	11.06
Nepali	10	201.79	20.17	15	717.67	47.78

(c) community or social causes.[31] A worker may be absent if he or she is sick or on a vacation or is simply in no mood to work. His or her absence may be authorised or unauthorised, wilful or due to some unavoidable circumstances beyond control. Absenteeism in the tea industry depends upon various factors which are uncommon to other industries. However, I shall compare here the rate of absenteeism of men and women workers of tea industry to see who are less committed and who are more committed.

In 1980 in Chandmoni Tea Estate the women workers of Oraon, Munda, Baraik, Saosi, Goala, Malpahari, Mahali Bhokta and Nepali were more absentees than their men workers. Only among the women workers of the Kheria, Meher, Gond, Goswami, Bairagi, Turi and Bihari absenteeism was lesser than that of their men workers. The rate of absenteeism of a woman worker was 24.65 per cent whereas for a man worker it was 20.22 per cent in 1980. Therefore, it appears from the study of absenteeism that men workers are more committed than the women workers (Table 26, 27).

However, the above statement will remain incomplete unless we discuss in depth the reasons for ansenteeism of both men and women workers. We must distinguish between the wilful non-attendance and non-wilful non-attendance of the men and women workers.

In general the plantation workers remain absent from their work mainly due to their addiction to liquor, social functions and festivals and illness. In case of women workers such absenteeism is mainly due to their household work and for looking after the children. The weekly rest day negatively affects the commitment of men workers. The workers get their wages on the day followed by the weekly rest day. Therefore, the workers, mainly the men, have the opportunity to spend a good part of their earnings on country-liquor. At least little less than half of the men workers remain absent from work for two or three days as they remain perpetually drunk for these days. Despite this fact the average rate of absenteeism among men workers is lower than that of the women workers (Table 26, 27). Three fourth of the total labourers are committed whereas one fourth of them are less committed. Generally the women workers belonging to the Ghasi

Table 26

Average Attendance and Absenteeism of Daily-Wage Men Workers in Chandmoni, 1980 *(300 Man-days in 1980)*

Adivasi and Caste	Number of Workers	Total Man-days	Total Man-days Worked	Average Man-days per Workingman	Average Absenteeism per Man Worker (in man days %)
Adivasi					
Oraon	69	20,700	16,737	242.56	57.44 (19.14)
Munda	36	10,800	8,304	230.66	69.34 (23.11)
Kheria	4	1,200	949	237.25	62.75 (20.91)
Meher	2	600	395	197.5	103.5 (34.17)
Baraik	11	3,300	2,416	219.64	80.36 (26.79)
Goswami	2	600	446	223	77 (25.67)
Saosi	5	1,500	1,138	227.6	72.4 (24.13)
Bairagi	1	300	260	260	40 (13.33)
Goala	3	900	821	273.66	26.34 (8.78)
Malpahari	7	2,100	1,699	242.71	57.29 19.10
Mahali	6	1,800	1,398	233	67 (21.67)
Bhokta	1	300	266	266	34 (22.33)
Korowa	5	1,500	1,175	235	65 (11.33)

Lohar	5	1,500	1,170	234	66	(22.00)
Turi	2	600	409	204.5	95.5	(31.83)
Ore	1	300	268	268	32	(10.67)
Ghasi	14	4,200	3,665	261.78	38.22	(12.74)
Caste						
Bihari	5	1,500	1,103	220.6	79.4	(26.47)
Nepali	10	3,000	2,698	269.8	30.2	(10.07)

Table 27

Average Attendance and Absenteeism of Daily-Wages Women Workers in Chandmoni,1980 (300 Man-days in 1980)

Adivasi and Caste	Number of Workers	Total Man-days	Total Man-days Worked	Average Man-days per Women Worker	Average Absenteeism per Man Worker (in Man-days %)
Adivasi					
Oraon	84	25,200	18,331	218.23	81.77 (27.26)
Munda	50	15,000	11,137	222.74	77.26 (25.75)
Kheria	5	1,500	1,282	256.40	43.60 (14.53)
Meher	1	300	294	294.00	6.00 (2.00)
Gond	1	300	146	146.00	154.00 (51.33)
Baraik	11	3,300	2,120	192.72	107.28 (35.76)
Goswami	4	1,200	1,000	250.00	50.00 (16.66)
Saosi	4	1,200	904	201.00	99.00 (33.00)
Bairagi	2	600	524	262.00	38.00 (12.67)
Goala	2	600	524	262.00	38.00 (12.67)
Malpahari	11	3,300	2,433	221.18	78.82 (26.27)
Mahali	7	2,100	1,580	225.71	74.29 (24.76)
Bhokta	3	900	657	219.00	81.00 (27.00)

Adivasi and Caste	Number of Workers	Total Man-days	Total Man-days Worked	Average Man-days per Women Worker	Average Absenteeism per Man Worker (in Man-days %)
Korowa	6	1,800	1,322	220.33	79.67 (26.56)
Lohar	6	1,800	1,211	201.83	98.17 (32.72)
Turi	2	600	445	222.50	77.50 (25.83)
Ore	1	300	240	240.00	60.00 (20.00)
Ghasi	15	4,500	2,702	180.13	119.87 (39.96)
Routia	–	–	–	–	
Caste					
Bihari	2	600	458	229.00	71.00 (23.67)
Nepali	15	4,500	3,596.64	256.64	44.36 (14.79)

and Baraik communities are least committed among all the Adivasi and non-Adivasi communities (Table 27). Though the Ghasis and Baraiks have come from Chotanagpur, traditionally they are not with an agrarian economic background. Perhaps their high rate of absenteeism is due to their maladjustment to the agro-based plantation occupational environment.

Among women the old workers are more committed than the middle-aged workers. The middle aged women are more burdened with household responsibilities. The young workers; specially the unmarried men and women; are more committed as they have less family burden.

There are some typical reasons for the women workers' absenteeism in plantation. In the rainy season (July-August) the rate of absenteeism is very high. There are two reasons for it. Those who possess cultivable land given by the plantation authority remain very busy with the Boro paddy cultivation during the rainy season. The other reason is that during this season quite often they suffer from various diseases like dioarrhoea, fever, gastro-enteritis, cholera, malarial fever, etc. Most of my informants have expressed such experiences. There is also another reason for absenteeism. The garden authority uses to give a plastic sheet and an umbrella to every worker once in two years. These are essential parts of the working life of the plantation workers as during heavy rain they cannot work without these. As the garden authority does not supply these two articles regularly some of the workers cannot attend the work during heavy rain. There are some other reasons also. Some of the old informants said that during the winter season their absenteeism is high because they suffer from cold. A few young women workers have expressed a different opinion. They usually remain absent in the winter season because it is a slack season in the tea plantation. As work load is not heavy in this period they can visit their relatives frequently who are also workers of other plantations in the Terai and Dooars regions. Besides, during the winter season they are very often busy with their household work such as paddy husking, cleaning and repairing their houses, constructing new houses, etc.

Besides, there are many other reasons due to which they remain absent from their work. When they themselves or their children suffer from illness, they cannot go to work. There are a few old women workers, who due to addiction to drinking, remain absent for 2 to 3 days in a week. Once in a week many of them remain absent from their work for washing clothes of the family members and for drying paddy for husking. Also sometimes they remain absent without any reason. Above all the most common factor for absenteeism is due to their visit to kinsmen living in other plantations of the region or due to their kinsmen who often come to visit them. In case of old women workers absenteeism is mainly due to their age and sickness, in case of middle-aged or young married women workers absenteeism is mainly due to some arduous household work or due to illness of their children. The committed workers regularly attend their work unless there is any strong reason for remaining absent from work.

It is seen from the above discussion that both men and women workers are more or less equally committed to plantation work. While turnover and extra leaf wages show that the women workers are more committed than the men workers, the latter appear to be more committed than the former in respect to absenteeism. However, factors behind women workers' absenteeism are various and are deeply rooted in the Adivasi culture. Such absenteeism does not depend entirely on the individuals' will but more on their cultural norms.

WOMEN WORKERS AND TRADE UNION

Participation of Women Workers in Trade Union

The workers of tea plantations in North Bengal initially participated in trade union activities only after the formation of Bengal Assam Rail Road Workers Union (BARRWU) in 1946. However it was a non-political union, but majority of the members were supporters of the Communist Party of India (CPI). The Congress was new in the trade union activities in this region, and in most of the cases it was sponsored by the employers only. In 1964 the first central trade union for tea plantation workers was formed in Jalpaiguri. It was later affiliated to the All India Trade Union Congress (AITUC). Its secretary was a wholetimer of the Communist Party of India and was an organiser of BARRWU at Dumohani.[32] The communist trade unionists were allowed to enter in the Terai region only in 1952 because of the general elections in that year. The union organisers of tea plantations used the chance to hold mass meetings in the labour lines in the protext of election propaganda. Ultimately the employers had to give recognition to the communist union to contain their workers only in 1954.[33]

At present there are two rival trade unions in the Chandmoni Tea Estate. These two trade unions are always in competition with each other, and they try to extend control over the workers. One of the trade unions is organised by the Congress Party which is locally known as Rastriya Chiya Mazdoor Congress (RCMC) and the other one is organised by the Centre of Indian Trade Unions (CITU) locally known as the Darjeeling District Chiya Kaman Mazdoor (DDCKM). This latter trade union is influenced by the ideology of the Communist Party of India (Marxist). The RCMC union was started in Chandmoni in 1950 and the CITU has been properly functioning since 1967-68.

The unions function through the garden committee and its office bearers such as president, secretary and treasurer. All of them are men workers of the plantation and none are women. There is no scope for women to occupy such positions. The top leadership is not of working class origin. The leaders hail from the Bengali middle class families or they are of the 'Babu' class origin. This is mainly due to the fact that the plantation workers are not in a position to handle the matters of trade union nor there is any attempt to train them to do so. The secretary of the CITU is a Christian wage-worker of Chandmoni. He hails from the Munda community. It has been difficult for him to get the backing and co-operation of the sub-staff who consider themselves superior to him. The president is a compounder of the tea estate, a Bengali Babu. In case of the RCMC union, a Dafadar is the secretary who belongs to the Oraon community. He has to rely heavily on the advice of the sub-staff and old people while performing his duties. The president of this union is also a factory worker of Chandmoni and belongs to the same ethnic group.

The CITU has its roots among the women workers of the Chandmoni Tea Estate whereas the RCMC union is less popular among them. Though there are 88 (39.82 per cent) women workers as members of the RCMC union seldom they participate in the meetings and in the decision-making processes. Whereas the CITU women members, whose number is 123 (55.65 per cent), are comparatively more active. A few of them take part in party meetings under the leadership of a woman named Manika Roy. This woman is the wife of the president of the CITU. She hails from a Bengali Brahmin family and teaches in a primary school. She has organised a Mahila Samiti in the Chandmoni Tea Estate.

The trade union leaders of the local committee of Siliguri select the secretary of the garden unit. In most of the cases it is through the common consensus of the workers but not through elections. The secretary is the most powerful person among the workers of the tea estate. He is entrusted with many responsibilities of the union who leads its members and is the chief spokesman to demand for benefits of the workers. Sometimes a second rank leadership may also emerge to mobilize the workers for mass meetings and hold line meetings to discuss workers' demands, etc. Such a second rank leadership is uncommon to this garden.

The trade union collects its funds from its members. The lion's share of the union fund comes from the union fees. The union fees for the RCMC is Re. 1 per month for each member. In addition, each member contributes Rs. 5 to the union fund at the time of yearly bonus. In case of the CITU the membership fee for each member is 25 paise per month along with the additional annual contribution of Rs. 5. The members who are monthly wage workers get higher annual bonus and therefore their membership subscription is also higher.

From the Table 28 it is seen that most of the Christian workers of Chandmoni are members of the RCMC, i.e., 82.22 per cent are members of this trade union whereas 17.79 per cent of them belong to the CITU. The Saonsars show a tendency towards the CITU membership. There are 227 (67.76 per cent) workers to the CITU and 108 (32.24 per cent) to the RCMC. Among the caste groups there is also high trend of CITU membership. About 95.84 per cent are members of the CITU while 4.16 per cent are of the RCMC. The old men and women workers are generally supporters of the RCMC union, but the members of the young generation are more inclined to take membership of the CITU, because some of them seem to be politically conscious. It is seen that 92 Christian Oraon workers are members of the RCMC

Table 28

Workers and Trade Union Membership, 1978-79

Ethnic Group	Number of the Union Members								Those Who are Not Member of any Trade Union			
	R.C.M.C				C.I.T.C							
	M	F	C	Total	M	F	C	Total	M	F	C	Total
Adivasi												
Oraon	60	54	9	123	24	24	3	51	–	2	–	2
Munda	18	11	5	34	35	31	1	67	–	5	–	5
Kheria	3	4	1	8	4	1	1	6	–	–	–	–
Meher	–	–	–	–	1	1	1	3	–	–	–	–
Gond	–	–	–	–	1	1	–	2	–	–	–	–
Baraik	3	1	–	4	16	10	3	29	–	–	–	–
Goswami	–	–	–	–	4	4	–	8	–	–	–	–
Saosi	1	1	–	2	3	2	–	5	–	–	1	1
Bairagi	–	–	–	–	3	2	–	5	–	1	–	1
Goala	–	–	–	–	3	2	–	5	–	–	–	–
Malpahari	2	3	1	6	6	6	–	12	–	–	–	–
Mahali	4	3	–	7	2	3	1	6	–	–	–	–
Bhokta	2	2	–	4	–	1	–	1	–	–	–	–

Contd..

Ethnic Group	Number of the Union Members								Those Who are Not Member of any Trade Union			
	R.C.M.C				*C.I.T.C*							
	M	F	C	Total	M	F	C	Total	M	F	C	Total
Ghasi	3	4	–	7	14	9	2	25	–	1	1	2
Korowa	–	–	–	–	5	5	–	10	–	–	–	–
Routia	1	2	–	3	–	–	–	–	–	–	–	–
Bhiyan	–	–	–	–	1	–	–	1	–	–	–	–
Lohar	4	3	–	7	2	3	–	5	–	–	–	–
Turi	–	–	–	–	3	2	–	5	–	–	–	–
Ore	–	–	–	–	1	1	–	2	–	–	–	–
Caste												
Bengali	–	–	–	–	1	–	–	1	–	–	–	–
Bihari	2	–	–	2	2	10	1	13	–	–	–	–
Nepali	–	–	–	–	16	13	3	32	–	1	2	3
Total	103	88	16	207	155	123	16	294	–	10	4	14

union and only 10 are members of the CITU. Among the Saonsar Oraon 31 are members of the RCMC and 41 are of the CITU. But there is only 1 Christian Munda as a member of the RCMC union while 8 are of the CITU. Among the Saonsar Mundas 33 are the members of the RCMC and 59 are of the CITU. In case of Christian Kheria 4 are members of the RCMC and 3 are of the CITU, whereas 4 Saonsar Kheria are members of the RCMC and 3 are of the CITU. However, it is revealed that majority of the Adivasis and caste groups have inclination towards CITU unionism. Out of the total of 515 workers only 207 (40.19 per cent) are members of the RCMC union and 294 (57.08 per cent) are of the CITU. The rest 14 (2.72 per cent) workers have not accepted membership in any of the unions; among them 10 are women and 4 are children. Among these women workers two declined to continue their membership in the union because they did not get any help from the organisation when they had faced social problems due to their inter-ethnic marriage. A few cases are given below. Sudhni Naik (22) a Ghasi woman, a worker of Chandmoni, married a Munda. She was a member of the RCMC union. But due to inter-Adivasi marriage she had to pay a fine to the Adivasi Panchayat and in this matter her union did not support or help her. She resigned from the membership of the union and discontinued the subscription. There was another reason also. Her younger brother Bhutan Naik (20) did not get promotion from child worker to the adult worker category, and the RCMC union did not help him in this matter. His brother also discontinued the RCMC union membership due to this reason. At present they both are not members of any trade union. Khuse Rai (46), a Nepali woman worker said that her husband had died on duty in 1974. But the management refused to pay any compensation and even his provident fund was not paid. Khuse who was a member of the RCMC union requested the union leaders for fair judgement but did not help her. Since then Khuse left the RCMC and at present she does not belong to any union. Similarly Marsha Munda (57) left the CITU membership because the union did not help her to recover her retired husband's provident fund. Rest of the women workers who were not members of any trade union left union membership due to some personal grievances.

The union involvement of the women workers is very low. The involvement of the members in the union is examined in terms of their evaluation of the organization and their participation in its activities. None of the women workers knows the actual names of the trade unions to which they belong. They can only recognize the emblems of the trade unions. Whereas sixty per cent of the men workers are well aware of it. In general they are less aware of the details functions of the unions due to their illiteracy and limited world view. The political ideologies as well as political functions of the trade unions are unknown to them. They do not know even the names of the chief minister of West Bengal, Prime Minister of India, etc.

The plantation women workers are not in a position to take active part in trade union activities because of the social conditions. As soon as they finish their work they rush back to their home for doing their domestic work. The men do not like them to keep away from home after their work is over. As a result, women workers find it extremely difficult to attend union meetings or to visit union offices. On most occasions, therefore, their membership in the trade unions is little more than nominal. However, if any dispute regarding their own jobs crops up individually they are very quick to ventilate their grievances as loudly as possible. In general issues, however, they depend on the men workers, join in the strikes and other activities with them as passive supporters.

Out of the total women workers of 221 only 10 (4.52 per cent) are regular participants of the unions, who regularly attend party meetings. The rest of them are very irregular in this respect. Among the 10 regular women participants of the union 3 belong to the Munda, 1 (one) to the Baraik, 1(one) to the Goala and 2 to the Nepali castes and the rest 3 to the Oraon. Out of the 221 women workers 211 (95.47 per cent) are the union members. The members approve the union, whatever its politics or performances, because they know that only the union is exclusively devoted to their interests, though a few (4.52 per cent) are of the view that union never serves their interest.

The informants were asked to name the most important of the four union activities, namely, economic bargaining, improving the working condition of the workers, building social solidarity and changing the political and social system of the country. Though most of them were unaware of the details functions of the trade unions they clearly knew certain specific functions. About 210 women workers told that economic bargaining was the most important function. Only about 5 per cent gave very vague opinion about the general functions. Similarly to a few women workers (6.78 per cent) union was meant to defend their service interests.

The plantation workers belong to the unskilled category except a few who can be accepted as semi-skilled labourers. They are mostly concerned with the wages but not with their long term benefit. They often issue strike notice to demand for bonus, specially before the Durga Puja. In August, 1978, September, 1979 and 1980 there were general strikes for bonus. During this period there were a few token strikes demanding the arrear money of the enhanced wages. Such decision over strike was taken at the meeting of the co-ordination committee of the tea plantation workers of West Bengal in Jalpaiguri.

In Chandmoni a situation of unrest existed in 1977 when the rivalry between the RCMC and the CITU was at its peak. Influence of political parties from outside the plantation aggravated the situation when a RCMC leader was murdered. One Bihari boy named Bhagawan Jha was responsible for the incidence. He was an active supporter of the CITU. For this incidence 7 men were dismissed by the authority. In 1978 there was a general strike for indefinite period on the bonus issue. It lasted for one month and twenty one days. The two rival unions were united and demanding for 12 per cent bonus. Lastly, the bonus issue was settled at 8 per cent. During the period from September 1977 to July, 1979 the manager of Chandmoni was a very ill-behaved person whose relation with the workers was very strained. In 1979, the workers gheraoed the manager several times and in July of this year they severely man-handled him and forced him to resign. In September, 1979, the workers called for a general strike for the bonus issue. This year they demanded for 16 per cent bonus. Finally it was settled at 9 per cent.

In Chandmoni the situation gradually improved when a new manager joined in November, 1979. In February, 1980 there was a general strike for 15 days demanding the arrear money of the enhanced wages and also the enhanced wages of the women workers at par with the men workers. In this year before the Durga Puja both the unions called for a joint strike for getting 20 per cent bonus. However, they succeeded in getting 12 per cent.

In the above strikes and gheraos the women workers also

joined although most of them were passive supporters only. They never took any active role except a few. A few names may be mentioned here who became prominent figures during the agitations. Bina Goala (50), Tetri Baraik (46), Raimoni Korowa (44), Etowary Oraon (39), Fulmoni Munda (30), Varshi Munda (48), Keso Munda (44), Khuse Rai (46) etc. quite often used harsh words to the manager. Bina Goala and Tetri Baraik who were members of the CITU exhibited emotional reactions with extreme aggressiveness. When provoked they became violent, but this was not due to their union involvement. It was only due to their aggressive nature.

There are two main factors which seem to be the genuine motive for the workers to join the trade union movement—the desire to get benefit of bonus and to get an arrear of the enhanced wages. In the transitional Adivasi society of plantation with a low level of technology the economic development is dominated by economic consideration and the workers' immediate objective is to attain higher wages and improved material conditions. Such a situation is quite different from advanced industrial society whose interests are many-sided and not merely economic. The plantation women workers have failed to join the trade union movement actively because they are not made aware of the trade unions' ideologies. They have no sense of lasting class consciousness as they are ignorant about their working condition, discrimination and exploitation. They are seen to be over-burdened with housework as well as plantation work. However, relation between the management and workers have changed considerably due to the trade unions' activities. Today the women workers have developed more contact with the management due to the changing relations.

The trade unions' functions are not only confined to the working life of the Adivasis but it influences their cultural life also. A few cases will reveal the role of union in the socio-cultural life of the plantation workers. Even in such cases women workers do not play any role in settling disputes. In 1978 Madan Bhokta (25), a Saonsar Bhokta, who has read upto class X, lured away Flora Soren (19), a Christian Kheria, who has read upto class VI. The boy lived in the neighbourhood of Chandmoni and did agricultural work. Flora's father was against this marriage; he is a Dawawalla and an influential member of the CITU. He called for a residential line Panchayat meeting and demanded Rs. 500 from the boy. As the boy was not a resident of Chandmoni the fine could not be implemented. Then Flora's father demanded baptisation of the boy, but the latter refused. Flora is a worker of Chandmoni and a member of the CITU. On her request the CITU leaders settled the dispute through a mutual agreement. In another case of inter-Adivasi marriage between Chamra Munda (20), a Saonsar Munda and Bengo Oraon (20), a Christian Oraon the RCMC and the CITU leaders settled the dispute in 1974.

There are generally two kinds of management-labour relationship. One is characterized by confrontation where the workers fight in every possible way to obtain their rights and benefits. The other involves a policy of accommodation in which management considers peaceful agreement as more advantageous. The situation in this tea estate seems to be more, one of accommodation, although some tension comes to the surface at times. Contact with the plantation owner is less possible as he lives outside, but the workers could present their grievances to the manager of the tea estate. The relationship of the workers with the present manager is overall good. He is quite popular among them specially among the women workers due to his pleasant behaviour. One factor of his popularity may be due to his long service first as a clerk, then as a assistant manager and presently as a manager and familiarity with the workers. The present manager personally knows most of the workers and calls them by their names. During the working hours he always moves with the workers and makes constant supervision of their work. The workers are at time afraid of him, but on the whole like him also.

The management's view is that the trade union leaders have ruined the innocence and submissiveness of the plantation workers. They have become lazy and arrogant due to the instigation of the trade union leaders. The manager said, "Now-a-days it has become difficult for the management to keep the male workers under the control and also to get committed work from them. Whereas the women are more disciplined and committed workers".

The Adivasi Panchayat in the Plantation

We have already discussed that the social structure of the

Chandmoni Tea Estate consists of multi-ethnic communities. This multi-ethnic social structure is controlled and maintained by the Adivasi-Panchayat. We shall discuss the role of the Adivasi-Panchayat in maintaining social control and cohesion among the various ethnic groups. However, the main concern here is to find out whether there is any role of the Adivasi women workers in the Panchayat. One can assume that along with the changing economic status in the power structure of the society has also undergone considerable changes. The study of the Panchayat of the plantation society provides an insight into the relationship between the multi-ethnic social structure and the distribution of power among men and women members of the society. It seems that there are : (1) general Panchayat—multi-Adivasi, (2) individual Adivasi Panchayat, and (3) residential line Panchayat—multi-Adivasi.

The Adivasi Panchayat is an informal institution for social control. It performs both jural and administrative functions as it can modify or prescribe customs for the plantation society. However, this Panchayat is not the same as the statutory Panchayat. There are two types of Panchayat in the Chandmoni Tea Estate, but none of them are permanent. There are a number of smaller Adivasi-Panchayats each meant exclusively for one community. Its composition is therefore ethnically homogeneous. The other Panchayat is multi-Adivasi composed of members from various communities. The latter Panchayat may be held at two levels : at the residential line level and at the plantation level. The Panchayat does not have any formal body like that of statutory Panchayat, and also there is no hard and fast rule for the formation of such Panchayat. The Panchayat is formed by a few Panches, i.e., persons. All the Panches are men. There is no place for women in the Panchayat.

The individual Adivasi Panchayat is exclusively meant for settling disputes within a particular community. It decides intra-community disputes, custody of children of separated couples and also settles disputes that arise out of inter-ethnic marriage. However, the smaller Adivasi communities of Chandmoni do not form such a Panchayat apparently due to their insufficient number. These smaller Adivasi communities settle their disputes through the general multi-Adivasi Panchayat. The multi-Adivasi Panchayat holds its session more frequently than the individual Adivasi-Panchayats. It decides cases relating to the general law and order situation in the Chandmoni Tea Estate. Cases such as theft, witchcraft, sorcery, inter-ethnic quarrels, inter-ethnic marriages, inter-religious marriages, etc. are also often settled. Sometimes the function of the trade union may merge with that of the multi-Adivasi Panchayat. Petty cases within a residential line may be discussed and settled by the male members of the various households living in that particular line. The role and function of various types of Panchayats will become apparent from the discussion of the following cases. Bengo Oraon (25) fell in love with Chamra Munda (28) and they got married in 1974. Chamra had already left his first wife. However, Bengo's father could not accept them, and therefore he lodged a complaint against Chamra to the Oraon Panchayat. In this Panchayat Bengo's father demanded Rs. 500 as a fine from Chamra which the latter paid to the Panchayat. The Oraon Panchayat took Rs. 200 and the rest was given to Bengo's father.

In this Panchayat meeting Daniel Oraon (Secretary of the RCME), Illias Oraon, Sammuel Oraon, Joseph Oraon, Manairam Oraon, Sanairam Oraon, Bandhan Oraon, etc. were present to settle the dispute but no women participated.

A case decided by the residential line Panchayat may be cited here. Koka Lohar (55) of Dibroo residential line of Chandmoni was notorious for rowdyism and addiction to liquor. Since long the neighbourers did not like him. In 1976 Koka brought in his home a woman named Noni Lohar with her four sons, and kept her as a concubine. Koka had already married and had a daughter who was also married. His daughter and son-in-law were staying at that time in the same residential line. The residents of the Dibroo line did not like it and they held a Panchayat meeting. In this meeting Dibroo Munda, Somra Munda, Jallah Oraon, Gondra Munda, Sitaram Naik, Bhulan Naik, Bhudhua Munda, Thepai Munda, etc. took active part. After prolonged discussion Koka was socially ostracised and he was asked to leave the residential line. The Panchayat also requested the management to implement the decision. Since then Koka started to live separately in an isolated place away from other residential lines. All workers of Chandmoni irrespective of any community discontinued social interactions with him. But he had developed close relationship with two other excommunicated families, that of Balkumari Majhi and Dharmadas Majhi. However, as Koka is a Sardar in Chandmoni he could exert his influence and command respect from his co-workers. This indicates the separation to some extent between social life and working life in the plantation. The Panches who decided this case were elderly men of various Adivasi communities. No woman participated in the Panchayat meeting as a member of the Panch.

A big general multi-ethnic Panchayat was held in Chandmoni in 1977. Balkumari Majhi, a retired Turi woman worker of Chandmoni was suspected to be a witch who lived in the Matigara residential line of Chandmoni. In 1977 due to an epidemic a large number of cattle died and many workers suffered from diseases in Chandmoni. Bisnath Bhokta a retired Sardar and some elderly persons of the same residential line sought advice of an Ojha who held Balkumari Majhi as a witch and advised them to drive her from Chandmoni. Then all the Adivasi men workers of Chandmoni held a Panchayat and decided to beat her to death or to drive her out from Chandmoni. The management of Chandmoni took up the case and suggested the Panches to let her live separately in an isolated place within Chandmoni. Since then she had started to live in an isolated place not very far from Koka Lohar's house. No women worker participated in the Panchayat proceedings although this case involved a retired woman worker of the plantation.

There is no fixed or permanent body of members of the Panchayat. Both old and young men may join and take part in the decision making process. However, initiative is taken by a few powerful men or Panches who appear to be self appointed. They decide what action should be taken on certain matter and then they inform the common men of their respective societies about the venue and time of the meeting. Generally meetings are held in the playground of Chandmoni. The women are deliberately excluded from such meetings as if they are unable to discuss and decide any social matter. The Panch, i.e., important men members discuss the matters in the Panchayat meeting and they participate in the decision. Women of the society have no place even today in the functioning of the Panchayat.

Traditionally, the common will of the community was expresed by the village Panch where the entire village community participated in theory. But in practice the Panchayat was represented by the elderly men of the village. Practically there was no role of women in the decision making process in the Panchayat. In the present situation in the plantation the women workers have also no role in the decision making process, they can only sit and hear the decisions. However, normally they do not even take part in the meetings. They can only join as silent audience. As the women have no role in the decision making process their political status has yet to be improved. The economic status of the plantation women workers has improved but at the Panchayat level they are yet to be accepted as full members having a say in the decision making process. Economic independence does not necessarily bring improvement in the power and privileges in other spheres of life.

References

1. Bhowmik, S., *Class Formation in the Plantation System,* Peoples Publishing House, New Delhi, 1981, p. 108.
2. Roy, S.C., *The Oraons of Chota-Nagpur,* The Brahmo Mission Press, Calcutta, 1915, pp. 68-75.
3. Bista, D.B., *Peoples of Nepal,* Ratna Pustak Bhandar, Kathmandu, Nepal, 1980, pp. 1-35.
4. *Report on the Survey of Labour Conditions in Tea Plantations and Tea Factories in India, 1961-62.* Labour Bureau, Ministry of Labour-Employment and Rehabilitation, Government of India, 1966, p. 22.
5. Griffiths, P., *The History of the Indian Tea Industry,* Weidenfel and Nicolson, London, 1967, p. 269.
6. Dalton, E.T., *Tribal History of Eastern India,* Cosmo Publications, New Delhi, 1973, p. 161.
7. Griffiths, P., op. cit., p. 271.
8. Bhowmik, S., op. cit., pp. 55-56.
9. Griffith, P., op. cit., p. 269.
10. Ibid., p. 277-278.
11. Ibid., p. 274.
12. Hunter W.W., *A Statistical Account of Bengal,* Vol. X (Reprinted), D.K. Publishing House, New Delhi, 1974, p. 166.
13. ILO, *Recent Development in Certain Aspects of Indian Economy-V,* International Labour Office, New Delhi, 1960, p.6.

14. Griffiths, P., op. cit., p. 285.
15. Bhowmik, S., op. cit., p . 59.
16. Griffiths, P., op. cit., p. 186.
17. Recently the management had taken back the paddy land given to the labourers for cultivation. This was part of the expansion programme of the tea estate undertaken by the management. The labour unions demanded recruitment of one person from each family which was affected due to this expansion programme. The vacancies created in this way was known as "paddy land demand vacancies".
18. *Indian Labour Gazette,* December, 1958, p. 441.
19. *Indian Labour Statistics,* 1962, p. 55.
    Indian Labour Year Book, 1965, pp. 51-52.
20. ILO, New Delhi, 1960, op. cit., p. 19.
21. *Report of the Central Wage Board for Tea Plantation Industry,* Government of India, 1966.
22. Bhowmik, S., op. cit., p. 94.
23. Ramaswamy, E.A. and Uma, *Industry and Labour,* Oxford University Press, New Delhi, 1981, pp. 14, 20, 28.
24. Sharma, B.R. , "Commitment to Industrial work : The case of the Indian Automobile Workers" in *Indian Journal of Industrial Relations,* 1963, 4(1), pp. 3-33.
25. Morris, D.M., "Some Comments in the supply of Labour to the Bombay Cotton Textile Industry 1854-1951" in *Indian Economic Journal*, 1953, 1(12), pp. 138-52 Thorner, D., "Casual Employment of a Factory Labour Force : The case of India 1850-1939" in *Economic Weekly,* 1957, Annual Number.
26. Morris, D.M., *The Emergence of an Industrial Labour Force : A Study of Bombay Cotton Mills 1854-1947,* Berkley, California, 1963.
27. Kerr, C., J.T. Dunlop, F.H. Marbison and C.A. Mayers, *Industrialism and Industrial Man,* Heinemann, London, 1960.
28. Lambert, R.D., *Workers, Factories and Social Change in India,* Princeton University Press, Princeton, N.J., 1963, pp. 82-83.
29. Form, W.H., *Blue-Collar Stratification,* Princeton University Press, Princeton, New Jersey, 1976.
30. Mehotra, G.N., *Studies in Industrial Sociology—The Indian Context,* Atma Ram & Sons, New Delhi, 1975, pp. 12-13.
31. Sinha, D., "Control of Industrial Absenteeism" in *Indian Journal of Labour Economics,* Vol. IV, No. 2 July, 1961 pp. 123-124.
32. Bhowmik, S., op. cit., pp. 142-143.
33. Griffiths, P., op. cit., p. 388.

Chapter 5

Women and the Social Environment of the Plantation

This chapter mainly concentrates upon the social life of the women workers in the Chandmoni Tea Estate with a view to show the impact of plantation industry on the social and cultural life of the women workers and the extent to which the traditional life-style has changed in this environment. I have discussed the changes that have taken place in the institution of family and marriage, familial relationships and austerity pattern, process of socialization of female children, process of social adjustment of the women workers in the industrial environment, nature of their economic contribution to the families, social status of the women workers and their general outlook.

FAMILY AND MARRIAGE AMONG WOMEN WORKERS

The Family

There are 276 families in the Chandmoni Tea Estate which can be divided into three types namely, nuclear, joint and unclassified on the basis of their size and composition. The nuclear families generally consist of parents and their unmarried children. The joint families consist of married sons and daughters living with their parents or sometime two married brothers living together with their sons and daughters. The unclassified type includes single member or more members consisting not of husband and wife but of some other relatives. Out of 276 families there are 208 (75.36 per cent) nuclear, 60 (21.74 per cent) joint and 8 (2.90 per cent) unclassified families. The nuclear families are of various types in their size and composition. The size varies from two to five and above members. The most common type of nuclear family has four members. There are 48 such families. Next in order comes the families with three members (44), five plus members (43), five members (39) and two members (34).

Table 29

Size of the Nuclear Family

Family Size	Number of Families	Number of Individuals
2	34	68
3	44	132
4	48	192
5	39	195
5 +	43	295
Total	208	882

The larger size is however not always due to greater number of children born to the couples in these families, but often some unmarried dependent relatives come to stay in these families as permanent members.

Table 30

Size of the Joint Family

Family Size	Number of Families	Number of Individuals
4	2	8
5	27	135
6	13	78
7	8	56
8	6	48
9	3	27
10	1	10
Total	60	362

The joint families consisting of five members are most numerous followed respectively by six, seven and eight members families. There are 27 families consisting of five members and 13 families consisting of six members and 8 families consisting of seven members and 6 families consisting of eight members. There are also 3 families consisting of nine members and 1 family consisting of ten members (Table 30).

There are 882 members in 208 nuclear families. Therefore, the average size of a nuclear family is 4.24. There are also 362 members in 60 joint families. So the average size of the joint family is 6.03. In case of the joint family there are a few typical large families. In such joint families sometimes married sons and daughters may live with their parents. There is the Ghardamad system where the daughters' husbands live with their parents-in-law. This system is prevalent in the families particularly who have agricultural lands of their own. The Ghardamad works on this land. Such system is very common among the Ghasis and Baraiks. Sometimes brothers' sons or sisters' sons are also seen living with their relatives in large families. In some cases where the couples have no son or whose sons are minors they keep Ghardamad to work on their land. There is also another reason for which Ghardamad works in the father-in-law's land. In a plantation, a daughter may be recruited if her mother is ill or retired. A son also may have a job in lieu of his father or mother; a daughter-in-law may have a job after her in-laws have retired. But the son-in-law will never get a job in a plantation after retirement of his father-in-law or mother-in-law. Other relatives may live with a couple if they do not have accommodation. Some times father's brother or sister who is working in the same plantation may also live with their nephew or niece, and some times minor brother and sister live with their elder brother or sister. Although there are a few joint families in this plantation the nuclear families predominate. The plantation's recruitment policy has strengthened such nuclearisation.

In the plantations of this region the labourers were often recruited in pairs by the Sardars of sometime they came in pairs in quest of jobs. Gradually they settled down in the new environment in pairs. The plantations offer equal opportunity to the women alongwith their husbands in the job market and consider a nuclear family as a basic unit to receive work facilities and other benefits. Certain facilities such as free quarter, free firewood, free cultivable land, ration at subsidized rates are given to each family. This naturally encouraged the workers to form nuclear families. In many cases these are the factors responsible for splitting up of large joint families into their constituent nuclear units.

Additional employment and filling up of the new jobs are done primarily on the basis of family units and not from the unemployed persons available within the plantation as such. The facilities given by the management is same for all categories of family units including single member units.

There are also other factors which induce large households to split into smaller one. Since 1970 in terms of the Tea Plantation Act, 1951, the management of the Chandmoni Tea Estate is providing some brick-built quarters to the workers. This accommodation is not sufficient for larger households. In such quarters there is only one room and a kitchen. If there is any family where two adult persons are workers, say for example, a father and a son who live together, they are entitled to get one quarter only. For instance Michel Kheria (40) lives with this married son Zirmeous Kheria (22) who is also a permanent worker. As they live together they are entitled to get one quarter only. But if Zirmeous establishes a separate family he will be provided with a separate quarter.

The functional role of the family has changed as the traditional mode of production has changed to a new type of production relation in the plantation economy. Work in the plantation has changed their economic activity from self-supporting peasant cultivators to wage labourers. Thus the family has changed from a unit of production to a unit of consumption. Traditionally, joint living was essential for joint and organised efforts for agricultural work and to support the family economy. But under the present situation in plantation society, joint-living to some extent deprives the workers of some of their due benefits from the garden authorities. Thus joint family, except under special circumstances, is disfavoured.

Though there is a predominance of nuclear family in the plantation society, nonetheless a close relationship with other primary and secondary relatives is maintained. Here the kinsmen and relatives who live side by side in nuclear families often help one another in times of need. In this feature of close kinship inter-dependence the plantation society differs from the other industrial society.

Marriage

In the Adivasi as well as the Nepali societies in the plantation marriage appears to be more a social contract based on individual choices, rather than a sacrament. A boy and a girl can marry according to their own will without prior consent of their parents. Sometime it may take place by negotiation. After marriage if a girl does not want to live with the boy, she can leave him and may live with another boy of her choice. In case of Christian Adivasis, marriage takes place in the Catholic Church as all of them are Catholics. The Church never objects to separation but does not allow bigamy. Among the Saonsar Adivasis divorce and remarriage of both men and women are not uncommon.

The consensual union, when a couple lives together without being married, is very common. In one sense we can call this as a prelude to marriage. The Adivasis also distinguish between marriage (Sadi) and consensual union (Rajikhusi). During the field work I have found that most of the couples have established new families on the basis of such consensual unions. As Adivasi man often refers to, "I am keeping her but our marriage has not yet taken place". But an Adivasi woman never says,"I am keeping him". If we look at the traditional form of Adivasi marriage we find that such consensual unions were not very uncommon in the traditional society.

Marriage among the two religious groups, Christian and non-Christian (Saonsar) is very common. Indogenous marriage is the general rule though there are numerous cases of inter Adivasi marriages particularly among the Mundas, Oraons and Kherias. In such a case the boy has to pay a token fine to the girl's parents. In the Chandmoni Tea Estate there are six cases of marriage between Oraons and Mundas. This type of inter-Adivasis marriage is socially permitted as it is thought that Munda, Oraon and Kheria belong to the same status group. But the inter-Adivasi marriages which take place between the members of two different status groups are considered as serious offence. This is generally settled through the Panchayat and sometime a serious conflict between the two parties may arise. In such cases the boy has to pay a heavy fine. About twenty years ago such couples were excommunicated.

Although marriage is strictly monogamous, sometimes polygamy also takes place. When the first wife proves barren, the man can marry for the second time. There are three such cases of second marriage in this plantation. Two cases are from the Mundas, one Christian and other Saonsar and the third case is from the Ghasis. In case of the Christian Munda the two co-wives are living together and in the other two cases the co-wives live separately. There is one incidence of a Lohar man, who has wife and a married daughter, keeping another woman with her children born of previous union. There are also some men who have extramarital relations with women living outside the tea estate. But such extra-marital relations are not socially accepted. The culturally approved formal marriage may be postponed, if the marriage formalities prove too burdensome at a given point of time. This happens among almost all the communities in the plantation. Therefore, they enter into consensual union (Raji Khusi) first and then, in most cases years later, they get married (Sadi) when their finances permit. In this formal marriage religious ceremonies are performed by a grand feast. Bhowmik has found the same trend among the Adivasis of the plantations of Dooars. He has reported that consensual union followed by marriage is not only found among the Adivasis but it is also noticed among other communities.[1] But I have found this custom only among certain low caste Nepalis and Adivasis. Such a practice is not prevalent among Biharis and high caste Nepalis, who are, of course, very few in the plantation. It was reported that there are a good number of instances where the couples were ceremonially married just before the marriages of their sons and daughters. If the parents do not perform their own marriage rituals their children do not get legitimacy. Marriage among the Adivasis in Chandmoni may operationally be used to indicate the common residence of a man and a woman exercising sexual rights and recognising the children born out of them.

In a negotiated marriage the father of a girl searches for a groom when his daughter reaches the marriageable age. If a suitable boy is found and if the boy's parents approve the girl then there will be an elaborate discussion for the fixation of the bride-price. The boy's parents have to pay the agreed upon amount of bride-price to the girl's parents. Among the Adivasis there is no system of dowry. Once the fixation of bride-price is over the pre-marriage celebrations take place associated with large consumption of rice bear (Haria) in the company of kinsmen, friends and relatives. On a fixed date the girl leaves for the boy's home where kinsmen and friends are also entertained with large quantity of Haria. There is another ceremony known as Kutumb-Khilana (engagement). If the girl likes the boy's family, after a few months, the relatives of both sides are called for a feast with drink. After these preliminaries are over the actual marriage ceremony is performed. If the girl does not like the boy's place or his people she may return to her father's house and may marry again. In such a case the bride-price is returned to the boy's parents.

There is another type of marriage, known as a Ghardamad system which we have mentioned earlier. In case the boy is unable to pay the bride-price, he lives with the in-laws as a Ghardamad and pays the bride-price by serving them in domestic work. In this tea estate there are 6 Ghardamads of the Oraons, 1 of the Baraiks, 1 of the Lohar and 6 of the Ghasis.

Plantation communities as a whole try to confine affinal relations within their occupational group from the neighbouring gardens. It is difficult to give the exact number of such marriages that had taken place as no record is kept. But it seems that now-a-days most of the marriages take place within the same plantation. It is due to some economic interests that they try to confine the marriages within the same plantation. According to the Adivasi workers, at present the job opportunities of a worker are very limited, and if a girl is married to a boy of other garden she will have to leave her job. Since there is no guarantee for getting regular job in other tea plantations, girls as well as their parents are more inclined to settle their marriages in the same tea estate. The Adivasi workers no more prefer to establish marital alliance with their native place although earlier they used to bring wives from there frequently. This has resulted into a discontinuity of social relations with the home land. This breach has been further augmented by factors like considerable distance, lack of proper communication and mental attachment with the distant kinsmen, changes in the ideas and values etc.

The data on marriage show that there are 83 inter-plantation marriages within the same occupational group. The couples are middle aged and young. About 28 young couples have married within the Chandmoni tea Estate. There are, however, 35 cases of marriage with persons of other occupational groups, namely, agricultural labourers, cultivators, wage-labourers in plywood factory, truck driver and cleaner, railway service holder, rickshaw puller, military service holder, etc. There are nine young couples who had married in their home land.

Inter-Ethnic Marriage

Inter-ethnic marriages are not socially sanctioned, despite a shift from the traditional kin-based rural environment to the new plantation environment. About 20 years ago cases of inter-ethnic marriages rarely took place as they were strongly disapproved. If such a marriage had occurred, the couples were excommunicated. At present the incidence of such inter-ethnic marriages seems to be on the increase. It seems that with the increase in communication and inter-action with society outside the plantation traditional ideas about marriage are rapidly changing and inter-Adivasi barriers are gradually breaking down.

The Adivasis of tea plantation are broadly divided into two status groups. One group which is considered superior consists of Oraons, Mundas and Kherias. Among them the Christians consider themselves superior to the Saonsars. The Oraons, Mundas and Kherias consider themselves culturally similar and have close social interactions among them, while the rest of the Adivasis are considered as socially inferior to the former group. This latter group of Adivasis have also close social interactions among themselves. Marriage among the Adivasis belonging to the same status group are socially accepted. If marriages take place between the Adivasi groups belonging to two different status groups, it is considered as a serious offence.

Although the population of tea plantations in North Bengal consists of multi-ethnic communities inter-Adivasi marriages seem to be quite rare in the plantations located in the interior regions. As for example, in Sonali tea plantation Bhowmik reports that there was only one case of inter-Adivasi marriage between a Munda boy and a Oraon girl.[2] As noted earlier in this plantation there are 20 Adivasi groups and 3 caste groups. We noted about 29 cases of inter-ethnic marriages among them during 1979-81. The Chandmoni plantation is situated very near to the Siliguri town. Urban influence on these heterogeneous communities appears to be quite strong. Besides, other factors play an important role in practising inter-ethnic marriage. The Adivasis who are few in number often have no other alternative but to take a wife from other communities. In recent years such marriages have become more frequent in this plantation and there is hardly any case of ex-communication. Even inter-ethnic marriages between Adivasis and caste group were found during my field work. Five such cases of Adivasi and caste marriages and 24 cases of inter-Adivasi marriages are given in Table 31.

Table 31

Inter-Ethnic Marriage in Chandmoni Tea Estate

Marriage Between the Ethnic Groups	Number of Cases
Oraon — Bihari Caste (Muchi)	1
Oraon — Munda	6
Oraon — Goala	1
Oraon — Lohar	1
Oraon — Kheria	1
Oraon — Gond	1
Oraon — Baraik	1
Oraon — Goala	1
Oraon — Rajbansi Caste	1
Munda — Ghasi	3
Munda — Bhokta	2
Kheria — Malpahari	1
Kheria — Bhokta	1
Baraik — Munda	1
Mahali — Ghasi	1
Ghasi — Lohar	1

Ghasi — Baraik	1
Bairagi — Bihari Caste (Khusbaha)	1
Turi — Bengali Caste (Kayastha)	1
Bihari Caste (Muchi) — Meher	1
Saosi — Goswami	1
Total Number of Cases	29

Out of 5 cases of Adivasi and caste marriages there are marriages between Oraon and Rajbansi, Oraon and Muchi (Bihari caste), Meher and Muchi (Bihari Caste), Bairagi and Khusbaha (Bihari Caste) and Turi and Kayastha (Bengali Caste). Out of 24 cases of inter-Adivasi marriages there are 2 cases of inter-marriage between Oraon boys and Munda girls, 1 case of marriage between an Oraon boy and Goala girl, and 1 case of marriage between an Oraon boy and a Lohar girl. There are 4 cases of marriage between Munda boys and Oraon girls, 1 case of marriage between Munda boy and Bhokta girl, and 2 cases of marriage between Munda boys and Ghasi girls. There are also 2 cases of marriage between Bhokta boy and Munda girl, and Bhokta boy and Kheria girl and 2 cases of marriage between Kheria boy and Oraon girl and Kheria boy and Malpahari girl. Among other inter-ethnic marriages there are 3 cases of marriages between Baraik boy and Oraon girl, Baraik boy and Ghasi girl and Baraik boy and Munda girl. Besides, there are marriages between Ghasi boy and Munda girl, Ghasi boy and Lohar girl, Mahali boy and Ghasi girl, Mahali boy and Oraon girl, Gond boy and Oraon girl, and Saosi boy and Goswami girl.

Inter-ethnic marriage, therefore, is widely practised in the Chandmoni Tea Estate so much so that often marriages between Adivasis belonging to two different status groups take place. However, such inter-ethnic marriages always involve a fine imposed on the couple. A part of the fine is given to the parents of the girl and the rest is taken by the Panchayat as it becomes the mediator between the two involved social groups. Thus the multi-ethnic society of the tea plantation has adapted to the reality of situation and has found means to accept inter-ethnic marriages through the medium of a fine, which is often a token of social sanction. Only in very rare cases ostracization is resorted to when

Adivasis belonging to two different social statuses inter-marry. In the Chandmoni plantation there were two cases of such inter-Adivasi marriages and offending couples were socially ostracized by the Panchayat. In one case a Lohar girl married an Oraon boy and in the other case a Munda girl married a Baraik boy. Both the couples were vanished from the garden. Payment of the fine which was imposed by the Panchayat could have neutralised the ostracism but as the couples could not pay, they were vanished. Sometime inter-union conflict may arise due to such inter-ethnic marriages, specially when the offending persons come from two rival unions. A few case studies of various types of inter-ethnic marriage that had taken place in the Chandmoni Tea Estate will reveal the reality of the changing situation.

Case I : Mariam Oraon aged 45 years is a Christian. She is working as a cow-herder in the Chandmoni plantation. She was born and brought up in the Ludim Tea Estate of Dooars and when she was about 18 years old she was married to an Oraon boy of the Ranichera Tea Estate of Dooars. After a year she fell in love with a Gond man who was a worker of the same tea estate. This man was a widower with a minor son. The man seduced her and continued to live with her in the same tea estate for a few days. Mariam's kinsmen became furious and haunded the couple out of the garden as the couple had breached the traditional norms of marriage. The couple reached Chandmoni tea plantation in search of job. Both of them were employed in the Chandmoni plantation. However, they have been accepted by the society of Chandmoni.

Case II : Bengo Oraon of 25 years was born in the Bagrakot Tea Estate, Dooars. When she was about 10 years old she came to the Chandmoni Tea Estate with her parents. After a few years she worked in the Chandmoni Tea Estate as a child-labourer and then as a permanent female worker. She has been working in this tea estate as permanent labour since 1971. At present her father is a permanent P.W.D. worker.

In 1974 she fell in love with a Munda boy of 28 years who was working as a garden Chowkidar. The boy was already married at that time. However, he left his first wife and started living with Bengo. The girl's father lodged a complaint against the boy to the Oraon Adivasi Panchayat of the plantation. In the

Panchayat meeting the girl's father demanded Rs. 500 as a fine from the boy as he belonged to a different community. The Munda boy had to sell his cow to pay the fine to the Panchayat. The Panchayat took Rs. 200 and the girl's father was given Rs. 300. However, the couple was socially accepted by the parties.

Case III : Flora Kheria is aged about 18 years and has read upto class VI standard. She hails from a Christian family. Her father is a health assistant of the Chandmoni Tea Plantation. In 1976 she was recruited as a permanent worker in Chandmoni through the CITU. However, she fell in love with a 20 years old Bhokta boy who had also read upto class V. Traditionally, the Bhoktas are considered as a community inferior to the Kherias. They started living as husband and wife, and there was no objection is from the boy's family. The boy's father is a well-to-do owner-cultivator and none of his family members works in the plantation. However, the girl's father lodged a complaint against the boy in the Panchayat of the Kheria tribe and he demanded Rs. 500 as a fine for breaching the social customs. As the boy lives outside the plantation and is not a worker in the plantation the fine could not be imposed on him. But the girl's father demanded for Baptisation of the boy, but the boy's father did not agree with the proposal. As the boy was not a worker of the plantation he was beyond the control of the plantation Panchayat. However, the conflict continued between the two families. Lastly, the couple with the help of the CITU settled the matter. However, the girl's parents have not yet normalised their relationships with the boy's parents.

Case IV : Somari Munda of 25 years age is an illiterate daughter of a Sardar of the Chandmoni plantation. She married a Ghasi boy of 27 years old who was already married. The boy read upto class IV. Their parents live in the same residential line in the Chandmoni plantation. Somari's father who was an influential person of the residential line lodged a complaint against the boy. In the Panchayat the case was decided and the boy had to pay a fine of Rs. 300 of which Rs. 100 was taken by the Panchayat and rest of the money was given to Somari's father. In this way the couple was socially accepted in the Munda as well as in Ghasi society.

Case V : Sudhni Naik, aged about 23 years, is an illiterate daughter of a divorced mother. She hails from the Ghasi community. However, she was in love with a Munda boy who was then a casual worker in the adjacent plywood factory. He came from Damanpur Tea Estate after the death of his parents. They started living together since 1979. As the girl married a Munda boy the RCMC union members considered it a serious offence as the Ghasis were believed to be inferior to the Mundas in the social hierarchy. Traditionally the Oraons, Mundas and Kherias did not take water from the Ghasis who by occupation were their drummers. The union members demanded Rs. 125 from Sudhani. But she could not pay the fine. The RCMC union debarred the girl from the membership and the couple was ostracized by stopping social interactions with them.

Divorce and Remarriage

We have already mentioned in the earlier section of this chapter that to the Adivasis marriage is mere a social contract rather than a sacrament. Consensual union is the general norm followed by a formal marriage. The Adivasi boy and girl can marry according to their own will, and such consensual union can easily break down at their will. If a girl marries a boy and after sometime she does not want to live with him, she can leave him and can marry another person. If the boy leaves her, she can marry again. If at the time of divorce they have got children, they mutually decide with whom the children shall live. This system is prevalent among all the Adivasis of the tea garden. The society allows a woman or a man to marry more than once. This custom is the same in respect of Christian as well as Saonsar Adivasis. Divorce among the Christian Adivasis is accepted by the church. But polygamy is strictly forbidden and the church may ex-communicate the couple. But among the Saonsar Adivasis polygamy is not an offence, it is only socially criticised. In the Chandmoni plantation there were six cases of polygamy in 1979. In two cases the co-wives are living together. Celas Barla aged 55 is a Christian Oraon and is a monthly rather worker of Chandmoni plantation. His first wife Magdalli Oraon was barren, that is why he took Varsi Munda as his second wife. Now the co-wives are living together without any conflict after the death of Celas in 1979. In the second case Koka Lohar aged 52, is a Saonsar and a monthly rated worker. He was married to Siben Lohar who bore her a daughter. After the serious illness of Siben by which time the daughter was also married, he married again an old Lohar widow who had also four children by her first husband. The two wives live together. In other four cases the co-wives live separately to avoid conflict. Bhulan Naik is a monthly rated Ghasi worker of 27 years old. He is a Saonsar who had married Asha Naik who was born and brought up in the Ludim Tea Estate, for the first time. After four years of their marriage Bhulan fell in love with Somari Munda and married her. His two wives now live separately in the same residential line. In the other case Chamra Munda, a Saonsar, aged 28, who is a Chowkidar was married to Mangri Munda for the first time and then he fell in love with Bengeo Oraon and started living with her abandoning his first wife. Now the two wives live separately in the same residential line and Chamra looks after both the wives.

Birsa Oraon, a Dafadar, a Saonsar and aged about 45 years was married to Jatri Oraon. They have five children. Birsa had some affairs with Etowari Oraon of the nearby Dukhuria basti, who was also a temporary worker of the Chandmoni Tea Estate. Finally, Etowari married Birsa as the second wife. Now Jatri and Etowari are living separately. Similar incidence of polygamy was found in the case of Birsa's brother Lal Oraon. Lal is 32 years old and also a monthly rated worker. He was married to Sonia Oraon for the first time and then married an Oraon girl, Sudhni, who was living in a nearby 'basti'. She is not a worker of the garden. His two wives live separately.

Marriage in the plantation society can be defined as elsewhere as a socially approved relation between a man and a woman. Pre-marital sex is a matter which hardly concerns the society unless the girl becomes pregnant. After payment of the agreed bride-price a date is fixed when bride goes to the groom's house and starts living with him. If she does not like the place, the man or his relatives, she can return to her parent's house. If she likes, she can marry again. In such a case the bride-price is returned to the groom's parents. No stigma is attached to such girls.

In case of concensual union the couple can dissolve their marriage at their own will and they can marry again. Adivasi men and women have considerable freedom to select their partners as well as to leave them.

In the plantation society this form of divorce is very frequent occurrence. In every household at least one or two cases of divorce may be found. But the practice of divorce has been gradually declining over the years. Members of younger generation look at this practice with disfavour.

Women and the Family Planning

The Adivasi women workers do not have any idea of family planning. In the plantation the rate of literacy of the women workers is very low, which is one of the principal factors of non-awareness of the birth control methods, resulting into high birth rate in the society. Low literacy level, lack of knowledge of birth-control methods are the major factors responsible for the high birth rate of the plantation women.

About 93.6 per cent of the women workers in the plantation are married. The average number of children per family is 1.6. This low average is not an indication of awareness of family planning as infant mortality is very high. They prefer to be mothers of more children as children can provide more economic support to the family as child labourers in the plantation. In this plantation even a few years ago children over 12 years were frequently employed in certain plantation jobs, namely, weeding, light hoeing, digging, etc. Grown up boys and girls are employed as permanent labourers under the rule of "permanent dependent vacancy filling".

Mothers are provided with the maternity benefits by the plantation authorities. This has become a positive inducement to the women workers to have more children and therefore, the birth-rate is high. Only two Christian Oraon women workers expressed some awareness to birth-control methods. Perhaps it is because their husbands are employed in the Military Engineering Service and in the Railways, and they have been influenced by their husbands.

WOMEN AND THEIR DOMESTIC WORLD: CONFLICT AND ADJUSTMENT

Authority in the Family

There is a correlation between class position and the authority of the males. In the lower strata, husbands are more likely to claim authority because they are male, but actually they have to allow more authority to their wives. Men of the upper strata generally assert less values of patriarchal authority, but in practice they manage to enjoy more power as they have more power resources. Women of the upper strata if they work, contribute a little to their family income. Their husbands are less dependent on the services of their wives and as a result husbands' position in role bargaining is much stronger.[3]

"The hierarchical structure of authority in the patriarchal joint family, which is based on the principle of superiority of the male members over the younger and female ones, is the most important instrument of social control. The rights and duties of the individuals are laid down to a great extent by this hierarchical order of power and authority, and their relationships with one another are defined within the limits delineated by the family authority, the male head of the family, legitimized and sacralized by caste and religion".[4] In the patriarchal society traditional male values are institutionalized in the family, economy, social and religious life. In reality power and authority of the Indian women as mothers is a consequence of the patriarchal family structure with its excessive emphasis on male descendants. "The status of a woman in the family is determined by the ranking of her husband among brothers, the length of the period she has lived in the family and the birth of sons. Only the birth of a son emancipates the Hindu woman from the situation of absolute subordination and helplessness, in which she enters the family as a young daughter-in-law".[5] Such "son-complex" is totally absent in plantation society. One reason may be that in this society both sons and daughters work and earn, and both of them are economically independent. In Hindu society father acts as breadwinner and if he is the oldest male member of the family, he then maintains a much more formal relationship with his children than the mother. He is, in addition to being the bread-winner, also the discipliner. This hierarchical authoritarian relationship is particularly observable in the father-son relationship; in the father-daughter relationship it is less pronounced. In Hindu society daughter is, above all, an economic and social liability for the father. In the plantation the daughters are not the economic liability but an asset to their parents as they earn from their childhood. The other reason is that there is no system of dowry for girls in marriage. So daughters are not burden to the parents, rather the parents get bride-price at the time of marriage of their daughters.

In the plantation society the functional role of the family has changed and the authority of patriarch had gradually diminished with the breakdown of larger kin-based joint families. The nuclear family units have emerged as independent self governing entities with changes in authority structure within the family units. Firstly, there is a change in the headship of the family. Traditionally, the eldest male members of a family used to be the head of the households. In the plantation situation, the quarter is alloted to the individual name of the male worker who may not necessarily be the eldest male member of the family. Thus the eldest member of the family gradually loses not only the economic control over the family but as well the power and authority. The power and authority generally rest in the hands of the earning members of the family. A large number of working women (nearly 80 per cent) in the Chandmoni Tea Estate expressed the view that as a consequence of their employment there is less conflict of authority between husband and wife. In the plantation society men are not only the providers. Their wives work and contribute to the maintenance of the family. As a matter of fact in many cases their husbands contribute a part of their income to the family purse as they usually spend most of their income in drinking.

In the plantation society men usually exercise less authority over women. The Adivasi women generally are exposed to very few restrictions. They enjoy much more social freedom than the Hindu women. Inclusion of women in plantation as wage earners is a criterion of considerably higher social status for plantation women, whereas the exclusion of women from all economic and intellectual activities was in India a criterion of status for the higher castes.[6] In plantation society plantation work becomes normal and essential component of married women's daily existence. The men, and perhaps the women themselves, have always seen women's part as one that derives from their position in the family. It is also important that the social institutions may affect women's standing within the family and outside the home in different ways. For example, the status of some of the Adivasi women like Ghasis and Baraiks is extremely low in their society, while the employment in the plantation enables them to bring the majority of the family income, and this has raised their status within the family. Women's status in the society as well as their power is low when they have low status both in economic and social spheres, and high when they enjoy relative authority in both the spheres. In the case of the plantation society from the point of view of authority there is greater equality among women and men than that in the rest of Indian society. Women's status, personal power and authority in the family are considerably high among the Adivasi plantation women workers. This has been possible for their crucial economic contribution as well as for the pre-existing values of near equality of women in the domestic sphere.

Thus a typical situation in the plantation society will read as follow. After marriage a son moves from his parental home and establishes a new family with his wife and children. The plantation authority provides him with a free quarter and he becomes the head of the household. The father, if alive, or the eldest male members of his old family loses control over the new family. When the extended family breaks down into single units, the father's authority tends to equalize with that of his wife; grown up children become more independent of parental control. Thus new ideas and values are absorbed more quickly in the families where young people hold the reins of the family. The wives got more opportunity to enjoy considerable authority in the family. The family and conjugal life have been significantly affected by the absence of the elderly members. The traditional kin bonds have also considerably weakened and the marriage has now become a more personal one than family affair. Thus many new ideas and values penetrate in the traditional social system through these family unit run by young husbands and wives.

Adjustment Between Domestic Life and Working Life

Every employed person is faced with the problem of defining the relationship between work and family in his or her life. If one is single or without children or dependent parents, this task seems to be relatively easy. Goode develops the idea that individuals "shop around" for "role bargains" in order to reduce their role strains. He feels that an individual's total role obligations are impossible to fulfil and there must exist various means to mitigate the role strains.[7]

Kinzer advocates that the general cultural norms may be mitigated by specific role relationships and specific cultural norms. These mitigating factors are: (i) specific cultural norms or legislation such as laws protecting the women workers, access to the educational system etc., (ii) husband's approval to his wife's working, (iii) means by which mother is relieved of continuous supervision of her children, and (iv) norms more often implicity than explicitly relating to the role of a working woman.[8]

The role conflicts occur when a person occupies two or more positions simultaneously and when the role expectations of one are incompatible with the role expectations of the other. The multiple statuses of a woman as a worker, as a wife and as a mother with her correspondingly multiple roles are each and in combination of potential sources of conflict. The role conflict may be of two types (i) intra-role conflict and (ii) inter-role conflict. The first one is associated with different expectations that others hold for a person, i.e., role set. The second one i.e., inter-role conflict is associated with the different expectations that are associated with a person as the incumbent of two or more positions, i.e., multiple roles.[9]

The women plantation workers occupy the statuses of woman, worker, wife and mother. They work for the economic necessity with the full knowledge of their husbands and children and associated with people who share their view. They seem to be happy with their job. They never feel inadequate and in kept as a wife and a mother. Most of the women workers in the Chandmoni Tea Estate hail from an Adivasi background. In Adivasi society the restrictions on movement of women are few. At the same time they enjoy economic freedom which also helps them to reduce their role conflict in their family as wives, as mothers and workers. Their working conditions, rules and facilities are also congenial for their work outside home. These to some extent help to mitigate the role strains of the women workers in the family. The women integrate their work and the family in an accommodative way. The role of wife and mother in a traditional situation is somewhat different. Here though they work, it is guided more by family needs rather than by rigid job requirements. The women workers of the plantation have low career aspirations and promotion facilities as well as job opportunities elsewhere are very limited. These factors also tend to make them more adaptive to the work and home environment. Their low aspirations and almost nil education also help them to adjust better to the family life than the educated middle class working women who are to compete in a shrinking job market and enter into a conflict with a rigid patriarchal family system.

In Hindu society, husbands are, traditionally, minimally accommodative to the day to day family needs, their primary commitment is to their work. But in Adivasi society particularly in plantation the situation is quite different. Here husbands are more accommodative to their wives. Most of them help their wives in household work including cooking, or in looking after the children.

Participation of women in economic activities is not a new phenomenon particularly in regard to the Adivasi women of the plantation. Family is the basic economic unit. The increasing nuclearization of the families in plantation has made the husband and wife relationships more crucial. Marriage here can be seen as a co-operative venture based on equal partnership. In such a situation mutual adjustment is vital for family stability, the women stretching their interest in work beyond the home while the men becoming more home centred. The situation has also influenced the relationship between parents and children at home.

In a typical industrial society there is a rigid separation between home and place of work. But in the plantation industry the situation is different. In a plantation both residential and working place are often close to each other. The working hours in the plantation are also routinised to accord with the day to day activities of the domestic life. The plantation women workers rise at about 5 a.m. to do household chores and prepare the breakfast. A 7 a.m. they have to go for their plantation work. After working in the field from 7 a.m. to 12 noon they come back home. They get a lunch-break from 12 noon to 2 p.m. when they prepare and serve lunch to their husbands and children. They again attend the afternoon work in the plantation at about 2 p.m. and continue to work upto 5.30 p.m. Then they return home and on the way collect some firewood from the garden. In the evening they prepare dinner and do the remaining household chores including taking care of the livestock.

A case study of a young working mother will reveal her daily routine. Asari Saosi (24), wife of Raghu Saosi (25) has two sons — the elder one is of 4 years of age and the younger one is of 11 months only. Asari said that she woke up at 5 a.m. and swept the house. Then she prepared tea and chapati. She and her husband took the breakfast when the sons were also fed. Then she cooked the mid-day meal in which husband helped her. Then she fed their goat. Husband also looked after the sons at that time. She went out for work at 7.30 a.m. along with the sons and took some tiffin for them. The younger son was kept near the working place in the garden and he was watched by the elder one. When the child required breast milk she fed him. At 12 noon she came back home and took lunch together with husband and son. Then she washed utensils and brought drinking water from the well when sons were looked after by her husband. At 2.30 p.m. she again went out for work along with her two sons and returned home at 5.30 p.m. Her husband collected some fire-wood and she cooked evening meal when husband also helped her. Then she fed her goats. In the evening they took meal together and went to bed.

The women workers those who have infants carry them on their back to the working place. The infants are laid down on a piece of cloth spread on the ground near their working place. While working they time to time look after them and breast-feed them if necessary. This facility given by the management avoids the problem of looking after the young children while they are away to work. Many families may not have elderly persons at home to look after the children. If the plantation authority had not permitted them to carry infants to their working place they would have faced the problem of raising the children. The women workers in plantation have to perform two roles, one as housewives and the other as wage earners while the men enjoy their leisure after the plantation work is over.

We have mentioned earlier in Chapter 4 that there is a creche in the Chandmoni Tea Estate for keeping the infants and children under six of the workers during the working hours. This facility has further reduced the burden of the mother to look after the children during working hours. Grown up children move freely within the garden premises with their playmates when their parents are away at work. The working condition in the garden offers necessary facilities and breaks to help the women to look after their children and attend to domestic duties. Though some husbands share the domestic burden with their wives it is the wives who are to tail harder. But this they do quite willingly and without any conflict. A conflict arises when the husband squanders away the money in drinks or runs after another woman.

Husband's Attitudes Towards Wife's Employment

It has been seen that in the working class families in the plantation although wives enjoy considerable freedom and authority in household matters the husbands symbolize the ultimate authority and power. This is but natural in a patriarchal society. In the joint family the father-in-law occupies the highest position of authority though he seldom wields his power without consulting his sons and daughters-in-law. However, a husband's attitude towards his wife's employment is important in understanding the role conflict of the working women in the plantation family.

It is seen that a high percentage of the husbands shows a positive attitude towards their wives employment. In the Chandmoni Tea Estate 98.19 per cent women workers state that their husbands want them to work, and only 1.81 per cent say that their husbands are against their working. But even in the latter cases there is no familial problem arising out of their working against their husband's attitude.

In general the overwhelming majority of the plantation

women workers live in a family atmosphere where positive attitudes are shown towards their jobs. In fact such a positive attitude of the husband helps not only to augment the income of the family but also to maintain cordial relations within the family. Even in joint families the parents-in-law accept the outside employment of the daughters-in-law as normal. It is not economic inducement alone that has helped to develop this positive outlook. This is also perhaps due to the traditional Adivasi ethos. Most of the Adivasis and other workers in plantation have come from an agricultural background where it is normal for women to participate in agricultural activities. The employment pattern in plantation also requires both men and women workers and if they are recruited from the same family it gives stability to the labour force. All these factors have contributed to evolve a norm in the plantation society where the employment of women is taken as something expected and natural.

The women workers do not seem to make any conscious effort to adapt to both the roles, one as housewives and the other as workers. In the conducive working environment of the plantation both the roles come naturally to them. The adaptation process is easy and devoid of trauma. Husbands of few women workers who work in organisations other than the tea plantation cannot help their wives in household work. Many of them get salary which is sufficient for maintenance of their families. But their wives do not like to discontinue their plantation jobs. This shows that they work not only for economic reasons but for other reasons also. These women are habituated to work in agriculture and the plantation industry provides them with a comparable agrarian occupational background. Because of the working class background their husbands often encourage them to continue with their employment in the plantation. The case of Parbait Oraon will probably illustrate this point.

Parbait Oraon (21) is the wife of Manairam Oraon (26). She was married to Manairam and came to the Chandmoni Tea Estate in 1973. Before marriage she was in Dardag, Ranchi. Her father was a small cultivator and she used to help her father in agricultural work. However, after a year of her marriage, she joined the Chandmoni Tea Estate as a temporary labour in 1974. Next year she was recruited as a permanent labourer as a permanent dependent of her husband. With the full approval of her husband and father-in-law Charoa Oraon who was a Sardar that her wages would help to support the family if she took the job on a permanent basis.

Sharing of Household Responsibilities

There is no uniform pattern of allocation of household functions and responsibilities among the members of the family all over the world. The allocation of household functions and responsibilities vary from society to society. These also depend largely upon the degree of change that has affected the institution of family and marriage due to the process of industrialisation. However, pattern of allocation of household functions and responsibilities between sexes differs in traditional societies as compared to industrial societies. In traditional Hindu society allocation of household functions and responsibilities is distinct between husband and wife. This distinction has given rise to specialization of duties among them, such as, while wife looks after all the domestic work and rearing up of children, the husband earns for the maintenance of the family. The former's duties are confined to the domestic activities while the latter's duties are largely outside the home. However, industrialization has brought certain changes in this traditional pattern by bringing co-operation of both husband and wife at the domestic level. Such a rigid distribution of duties between husband and wife is not distinctly found in Adivasi society in plantation. In the plantation society, as said earlier, both husband and wife work together and most husbands equally participate in domestic activities. Thus they share each others' economic and domestic responsibilities.

The sharing of household responsibility is principally found in the spheres of three domestic activities: handling of family purse to meet regular expenses, performance of daily domestic chores and looking after the children. Besides, planning for the future and certain decisions on crucial matters which may appear from time to time need to be taken. The data on these aspects were collected from the women as well as some men who are closely involved in the management of the family.

It is natural that when the wife is working as wage-earner she has a dual burden to carry. If the husband does not share the domestic responsibilities, tensions and ultimately rift may follow between a husband and wife. It is found that about 71 per cent of the husbands help their wives in domestic activities. In the plantation society doing the domestic chores and looking after the children do not affect the dignity of the husband. But probably this is a feature common to the working class where both men and women work as wage labourers.

Decision Making

One of the indicators of status of women is whether they play an effective role in the decision-making process in the family. To elicit information on this subject we put the question before the Adivasi and Nepali women — "Do you agree that the women should have a say in important matters regarding the family"? About 89 per cent of the women workers replied in affirmative. Seven per cent of the respondents replied that they did not have any role in making decisions for their families while 4 per cent gave vague answers. The latter group of women mainly belongs to the age group of 45-55 years and they are illiterate. When the same question was asked to men, 87.62 per cent of them were of the opinion that their wives should have a say in important matters regarding the family affairs. The rest 12.38 per cent disagreed, most of whom belong to the Nepali castes. This shows that the majority of plantation women do want equal participation in the decision-making processes of their families. Though majority of the working women desire equal share in decision-making, in actual practice this is enjoyed by a very few of them. In certain vital issues in the family like marriage and education of sons and daughters, husbands usually unilaterally take the decision. Wives' opinion is not much valued. But wives take the major decisions regarding the day to day family expenditure, domestic activities, etc. As the wives spend all their wages for the maintenance of the family they have a greater say in the day to day affairs of the family. Most of the husbands spend a part of their earnings on drinking rice-beer (Haria), and they generally do not interfere with their wives' earning. The wives generally do not object to their drinking as the drinking of rice-beer (Haria) is one of their traditional cultural habits. The quarrel may arise in case of excessive drinking. A few cases will illustrate the decision-making processes in the Adivasi family.

Gita Munda (25) and her husband Gondra Munda (29) are workers in Chandmoni. She has been working as a labourer since 1972 and her husband is a Boidar who earns about Rs. 300 per month. Their three sons are studying in the St. Mary's Convent School at Siliguri for which they spend Rs. 150 per month. Gondra hands over Rs. 250 per month to his wife and she controls the family budget. She is living in a joint family consisting of her parents-in-law, sister-in-law and brother-in-law. The sister-in-law and brother-in-law are also permanent workers of Chandmoni who contribute to the family income. She likes to live in a joint family because joint family usually gives better protection to women and children. Gondra enjoys the highest authority in the family, in the decision making process in relation to the household affairs and the education of their sons. Gita always tries to obey him. In all the decisions of crucial matters she is always consulted. Gondra and his sister usually do the weekly marketing at the Matigara Haat. Generally Gita does not like marketing. Sometimes conflict arises in the family front. Gondra is not addicted to drinking but occasionally when he drinks Gita picks up quarrel with him. Gondra tried to give up drinking as his wife does not like it at all. In this case it seems that both the husband and the wife are trying to adjust themselves conceding their self-interest every now and then in order to build a happy family life.

Economic Contribution

It has already been stated that the occupational status of husband and wife is same as most of them are daily wage workers. There are a few men who receive monthly wages, and, therefore, their occupational status is slightly higher than that of a daily wage worker. The number of such workers are 55 out of a total work force of 515. Income of both husband and wife is more or less same, barring wage-cuts due to absenteeism, illness etc., except that of monthly rated workers.

To get an answer to the question, why the women have taken up employment in plantation, all the women workers of the Chandmoni Tea Estate were asked "Why did you take up this job?" Out of 221 women workers 216 (97.74 per cent) replied that they had accepted the employment due to the economic need of the family, and only 5 (2.26 per cent) women workers expressed that they had taken up the job to supplement their family income. About 41.63 per cent of the women workers hand over their wages to their husbands. Out of 221 women workers 53 (23.98 per cent) women keep their earning with them and spend the entire amount to purchase food and other necessities for the family. These women workers manage their family budget themselves. They generally have husbands addicted to drinking. As such husbands contribute little of their income to the family purse, their wives have to take entire economic responsibility of the family. Those husbands who do not spend much money on drinking do not always give their earnings to their wives. In many cased both keep their earnings separately themselves. As many as 30.77 per cent of the plantation women workers jointly manage the family budget with their husbands (Table-32). They belong to the age group of 25-55 years and hail from communities like Oraon, Munda, Bhokta, Kheria, Ore, Mahali and Malpahari. In case of 92 women workers out of 221 the husbands control the family budget. They belong to Nepali castes, Ghasi, Baraik and Turi, and Lohar Adivasi groups. A few widow workers control the family budget themselves. However, in most cases shopping of food materials and other goods necessary for the family is done jointly by husband and wife in the local Matigara Haat held every Tuesday. More than 64.00 per cent women workers join their husbands in this weekly event. In rest of the families either the wife or the husband goes to the market alone. However, on the pay-day the husband usually draws his wage as well as that of his wife's. More than 65 per cent of the husbands were found to draw their wives' wages, and then after doing some minor shopping in Gudri Haat (local Haat) most of them handed over their wife's wages to them. It is generally seen that a part of the men's wages are spent in drinking rice-beer (Haria), or country liquor (Daru) and in smoking. Thus it is found that the women are the primary bread winners of the plantation family.

Table 32

Management of the Family Budget

Person Who Manages the family budget	Number of women workers	Percentage
Woman herself	53	23.98
Husband	92	41.63
Both husband and wife	68	30.77
Some other relatives	8	3.62
Total	221	100.00

Child-care and Socialization Process

Socialization is the process by which the young human being acquires the values and knowledge of his group and learns the social roles appropriate to his position in it.[10] The family is the primary institution which provides an environment to the young members to get socialized. The society at large, provides them with a wider environment to interest with others and grow into full members of the society.

Parents play a vital role in the socialization process of their children. But the woman's biological 'destiny' as mother becomes a cultural vocation in her role as a socializer of children. In bringing up children, plantation woman achieves her main social definition. However, the cultural allocation of roles in bringing up children and limits of its variability are not the essential problems for consideration. What is much more important is to analyse the nature of the socialization process itself and its requirements. The nuclear family is centred around the two-generational hierarchy between parents and children.

Plantation society has a settled population that is born, grows up and continues to live in the plantation environment. Children, when they grow up, often follow the foot-steps of their parents in so far as employment in the industry is concerned. The children, therefore, from their childhood share an awareness of the common problem of how their future life would shape up.

Among the workers of tea plantations child rearing is not

much of a practical problem as it is among the urban middle class working mothers. The workers in a plantation generally live within a community of kinsmen, though most of them live in separate households. Some old kinswoman may be asked to keep an eye to the children when their mothers go out for work. Sometimes old and retired parents look after the toddlers. Nursing infants are often carried on the back of their mothers to the place of work. A mother may also keep the infant in the garden creche, which most of the woman do not do, as they said "babies are not properly cared for there".

As noted above the socialization of the children is greatly influenced by the plantation environment. From the very childhood the children watch their parents doing different kinds of plantation work and when they become adolescent — the time to be employed as 'child labourers", they are quite acquainted with various types of plantation work.

The mothers carry the infants on their back to the working place and the elder children, specially the girls, accompany them. They look after their tiny brothers and sisters while their mothers remain busy with the work. Sometimes they also help their mothers in plucking and weeding; little girls collect dry twigs from the garden for daily cooking. The children also get some sort of training from hearing the frequent discussions on work among adult workers as well as from the instructions given by the Sardars to their mothers. The nuclear family with its limited number of members and a working mother necessitates the girls to do the household work. The girls from their very childhood get used to do the day to day household work along with their mothers and help her in cooking, cleaning utensils, looking after young brothers and sisters and fetching water from the well. From childhood till they are married the girls move freely with boys and girls and thus learn the mystery of sex life. Cases of casual sex affairs, with boys are not infrequent among adolescent and young girls.

Both the parents share the responsibility of their children. Being the lower class working people the plantation workers do not prepare their children for an ordered and achievement oriented life. Their ambition is very limited which is to get a job for their children in the plantation. They do not wish to make the process of life more complicated by making futuristic plans for the children. This may be one of the reasons for not encouraging their children to go for schooling.

In the Adivasi society of the plantation girls are socialized in their role of male dependency which continue even after marriage and they have a family of their own. Thus the values, norms and patterns of behaviour are transmitted from one generation to the next.

The Adivasi women in the plantation do not suffer from a "son complex" as has been mentioned earlier. They treat their sons and daughters equally. Even in matters of vital importance like employment, choice of a partner in marriage, etc. they are not discriminated. However, in the case of education, the parents show discrimination between sons and daughters. The standard of literacy among boys and girls is quite low as mentioned earlier. But whatever weightage is given to schooling it is primarily meant for boys. About 95 per cent of women workers interviewed by me did not intend to send their daughters to school. In most cases the plantation women workers are illiterate and it is natural that they do not want to educate their daughters. They hold that female education is not necessary for employment in the garden as well as for raising a family. But, in choosing a career in tea plantation women workers, in general, are willing to give equal encouragement to their sons and daughters.

On the whole in the socialization process the plantation family reinforce the 'gender roles', that is, the cultural definitions of the traits and behaviour that are appropriate for men and women. The process of socialization of plantation women builds a poor self-image for themselves. The process also leads to relate them with the men-folk in the family in terms of dependency, a symbol of which is to identify the women in terms of their husbands, rather than by their own names. The women are socialized and values instilled in such a way that they accept, without a murmur, their exploitation by the men-folk. The patriarchal family system, the lack of education, dependency, role differentiation and inferior position in the political system and in trade union help to create a social environment in which inequality between sexes is perpetuated. Economic freedom has done little to mitigate this position.

Status of Women in Plantation

In studying the status of women in a plantation society we must study the complexity of roles which the plantation women perform in socio-economic, cultural, religious and political fields. We have already seen the role performance of women in these spheres. The question that looms large is that whether economic emancipation of women workers has correspondingly elevated their status in the society or not.

The plantation society is a heterogeneity of Adivasis and castes. Traditionally speaking, in caste society the status of women is generally lower, whereas in Adivasi society it is relatively higher. One of the factors which contributes to a higher social status of women in Adivasi society is the economic role that they perform as wage earners.

It will be wrong if it is assumed that the plantation women enjoy equal rights and privileges with men. It is true that the Adivasi and Nepali women workers suffer few restrictions in their society. They can select their mates and can leave their mates as and when they like or they can marry again. Above all there is no system of dowry in their society. Only the system of bride-price is prevalent among them. If the groom is unable to pay the bride-price he has to live in the girl's family for a certain period and has to perform the domestic duties in his father-in-law's house. Such system of Ghardamad also refers to some kinds of higher status of women in the Adivasi society. But still Adivasi society is male dominated and women are treated as a commodity. The wife is often referred to as the "kept" by the husband but a husband is never referred to as a "kept" by the wife. Marriage being easily dissoluble the children may remain in the custody of mother or father as may be agreed upon. In many cases the children stay with their mother and when she remarries the step-father accepts her children as his own. In cases of remarriage of a woman, there are 22.17 per cent of cases where a woman with children remarried and the new husband had accepted her children in the family fold. This has been possible because the woman also contributes her wages to support the family.

The overall occupational status of the women workers is lower than that of the men workers. Although wages of men and women workers are equal today, even a few years ago the latter used to receive lesser wages. Unequal opportunity in the occupational hierarchy, that is, women are never made a sub-staff, renders them a lower status vis-a-vis the men. Women always work as daily-rated workers. They are not promoted to the position of the monthly rated workers, sub-staff and supervisory staff.

Plantation women workers have no role in the decision-making processes in connection with theft, witchcraft, inter-ethnic marriage, inter-ethnic conflict, etc. which are decided by the Adivasi Panchayat of the plantation time to time. The women do not have any voice in the Adivasi Panchayat.

Trade union leadership from the women workers of plantation has not yet emerged. Although women workers are members of the trade unions they hardly participate in the regular union meetings. But sometimes they take aggressive roles and join procession, demonstration, etc. Marginal participation in the union activities does not indicate that they have power in influencing the decisions of union leaders.

The educational attainment of plantation women workers is very low. Generally the level of literacy of the plantation workers as a whole is very poor. In case of women workers this is almost nil. This has further helped to perpetuate the lower status of women workers. The women workers are totally ignorant about the role of modern education in improving the status of women.

It is seen that though apparently plantation women workers enjoy considerable freedom of action their status when compared to men, appears to be low. Economic contribution has not helped to raise their status so as to make it equal with men. Their status is comparable to that of landless families in agricultural society because, in both cases, the products of their work are expropriated by their husbands.

Social Interaction of the Women Workers and Their Outlook

Tea plantations are usually situated in remote areas and the workers live within the boundries of the tea plantations. They have minimum connection with the outside world.

But the Chandmoni Tea Estate is situated near the Siliguri town. Workers interaction with the outisde world is greater than that of the workers of the interior plantations. The society of Chandmoni has undergone some changes but by and large it has remained traditional. The young boys and girls have changed styles of their dresses. They occasionally visit Siliguri town. The old and the middle aged women mostly remain confined within the tea garden. Their interaction with the outside world is very limited. They only meet the outside people in the local weekly market (Haat). The Haat is the place where the men and women workers meet with their relatives, friends and non-Adivasi people. It probably relieves the workers from the boredom of garden life and that is why they look forward to the market day. Everything of daily necessities and fineries are available in the Haat. This market day, held on every Tuesday, is also the weekly holiday of the neighbouring tea gardens, namely, Chandmoni, Matigara, Kamala, Sanyasi, Kiran Chandra, Hind, Singhijhora, Sahabad, etc. of the region. Many workers from the neighbouring tea gardens come and assemble at a particular spot in the Haat where they drink, gossip and exchange information with one another. Many marriages are negotiated in the Haat. It is also a place for romance for the young boys and girls. Many of the workers come to the Haat for drinking rice-beer (Haria) and country-liquor (Daru). Now-a-days the young women workers seldom take rice-beer (Haria) or smoke. Many of them come only for enjoyment and relaxation. Haat is perhaps the only place of contact with the outside world particularly for the older generation of workers. But the young girls and boys are fond of cinemas who frequently visit town for this purpose. Besides the weekly Matigara Haat there is also a local Haat which is held on the pay-day of the garden labourers, i.e., on every Monday. Readymade garments, fresh vegetables, fish and various household goods are sold here.

The young girls are more fashion-conscious than the old ones and the Nepali women are more fashion-conscious than the Adivasi women. In Chandmoni the women are not so conservative like the women workers of other gardens situated in the remote areas of Terai and Dooars. As for instance the situation in the Sonali Tea Estate of Dooars is different. Here the Oraons, Mundas and Kherias may dine with each other but generally not with any other communities. The concept of pollution has also touched them similar to the Hindus. Food is regarded as polluted if touched by anyone not in their common status group. Womenfolk are more orthodox in these matters. They do not take food or water at the market, no matter how hungry or thirsty they are.[11] Such a situation is rare in Chandmoni. The women here do not maintain such a pollution concept regarding food. They are not so orthodox, they eat and drink food touched by persons belonging to other status groups. Even they eat food in the Haat and interdine with Bengalis and Biharis. Inspite of this fact the Adivasi women workers appear to be conservative in regard to their dresses. Except a few girls, they use their traditional dress even today. The upper part of their body is covered with a blouse and a piece of cloth is wrapped round their waist reaching upto the ankle. Only a few Adivasis and Nepali girls wear Saris when they visit town and relatives of the neighbouring plantations.

The plantation women live within their own community, with their traditional beliefs and customs. They are ignorant of the changes that are taking place in the outside world. Plantation women seem to be more conservative than men. Some thirty years ago they were totally isolated from the rest of the world. In case of men such conservatism is breaking down rapidly as they come in contact with the outsiders more often. But in the case of women such isolation is also breaking down but at a slower pace. This is mainly due to their increasing participation in the trade union activities though they are very poorly represented at this point of time.

Among the Adivasis drinking and smoking are very common among both men and women workers. However, now-a-days young women workers are less addicted to drinking. Even some of them totally abstain from drinking and smoking. Perhaps they have been influenced by the upper caste women whom they frequently see in the market and the town.

Though some plantation workers have connection with town, yet most of the women workers live in relative isolation from the rest of the world.

The plantation women are less conscious about their living condition as well as their working condition. In most of the houses there is an absence of furniture. Those who are a bit affluent can only afford to have a wooden or string cot, and one or two wooden chairs. They are used to sleep on the hard floor.

The outlook of the plantation women workers can be judged from their low level of literacy. They have no idea about the need or importance of women's education. So they do not encourage their daughters to go to schools. Their knowledge about outside world is also very poor. The women workers, specially those who are older, do not know the name of the country in which they belong. Most of them refer to the Darjeeling region as belonging to Bhutan. The reason behind it is that when they were brought to this region they were told by the recruiting agent that they were to go to Bhutan. Old women hardly know the name of the Prime Minister of India or the Chief Minister of West Bengal. Now-a-days due to the compaign of the trade unions the young women workers are familiar with these names. Their spatial movement, if at all, is restricted to Siliguri, Jalpaiguri and a few tea gardens of Terai and Dooars. Occasionally they visit their relatives during their yearly vacation. Tea garden is the only universe for them. Thus they remain in an under-dog position and have become prisoners to a self-perpetuating system in which it is difficult to come out and improve their condition.

References

1. Bhowmik, S., *Class Formation in the Plantation System*, Peoples Publishing House, New Delhi, 1981, p. 121.
2. Ibid., p. 124.
3. Goode, W.J., The Family, Prentice Hall of India (Private) Ltd., New Delhi, 1966, pp. 74 -75.
4. Mies, M., *Indian Women and Patriarchy,* Concept Publishing Company, New Delhi, 1980, p. 92.
5. Ibid., p. 103.
6. Ibid., p. 30.
7. Goode, W.J., op. cit., p. 109.
8. Kinzer, N.S., "Socio-Cultural Factors Mitigating Role Conflict of Buenos Aires Professional Women" in R. Rohrlich-Leavitt (ed.), *Women Cross Culturally,* Mouton, Hague, Paris, 1975, P. 185.
9. See Merton, R., *Social Theory and Social Structure,* Free Press, Glancoe, Illinois, 1963, p. 269 for ROLE SET in which he defines it as that complement of role relationship which persons have by virtue of occupying a particular status.
10. Goode, W.J., op. cit., p. 10.
11. Bhowmik, S., op. cit., pp. 109-110.

Chapter 6

Summary and Conclusion

Research on women is not new but the studies offer a variety of concern with sifting emphasis and perspectives depending on one's theoretical orientation, changing situation, etc. These shifts in emphasis and approach have to do with trends in current thinking on specific issues relating to the society as well as to women in particular. The emphasis has sometimes been on inequality, on human rights and social oppression, on economic participation etc. The anthropological and sociological studies on women put much emphasis on kinship and marital adjustment. Recently they have sifted to the position of women in society with their changing role, status and attitudes. Research on women's role and opportunities in economic activities have remained marginal. At present we know little about Indian women in particular. Most of the social researchers either exclude Indian women from their analysis or they focus only on a limited sample of women who are not exactly the representative of Indian society. Most of the studies are concentrated on the educated urban middle class working women. However, there are only a very few sociological studies which examine women's attitude to work in a particular occupational context in a systematic manner. While social anthropological studies did occasionally note rural women's economic roles, they failed to examine any change, either quantitative or qualitative, in women's participation in economic activity. The researches on women in India indicate that prior to 1950's the focus was primarily on general surveys on women's role and status within the narrow perspective of family, kinship and community with education occupying the second position. Social anthropological studies on women in India are basically on family. Some of the studies clearly indicate an integral relationship between roles and status and nature of social stratification.

The research on women's roles and opportunities in economic activity has remained marginal. Anthropologists and sociologists surprisingly have ignored the major role played by women in industry and the manners in which they are being affected by the process of modernisation. They occasionally note industrial women's economic roles but they have failed to examine any change. The studies done on women from various perspectives like the status and roles in the society, employment in new profession, their position, etc. have considerably ignored to study the women who constitute an important part of industrial workforce. In the study of industrial anthropology and sociology women have been neglected for quite a long time. The role of industrial women workers, their adjustment to industrial environment, their attitudes and behaviour patterns, promotions and other facilities enjoyed by them, their relationships with the employer and other employees, etc. have not yet been dealt with proper attention.

The purpose of the present study is to investigate the factors responsible for plantation women workers to enter into the labour force and to find out how their industrial employment affects their behaviour patterns and life-styles. The tea plantation industry has a distinct form of productive organisation which gives rise to certain specific social relations. This particular study emphasizes the role of tribal women in the productive process of plantation system, their life and work outside the family in employment and their life and work within their family.

There are a large number of women who primarily derive their livelihood from working in tea plantation industry of West Bengal either as "free" wage labourers, often on a regular basis and sometimes on a seasonal basis (bigha labour) or they are permanently bondaged to a particular planter mostly along with their menfolk. These women generally belong to illiterate, scheduled tribes and backward communities. Invariably they work for longer hours than their men both in paid work outside their home and unpaid household work. These tribal women are always found working for a greater number of hours even where non-household is concerned. Often they are permanent employees of tea plantation and always attached labourers. They are mostly engaged in semi-skilled non-manual work, often in plucking in tea plantation. At present most of them are settled permanent labourers for three or four generations. So the question of "economic displacement" as well as "cultural strains" are not applicable to them. They have witnessed many changes in their economic conditions and life styles due to the shift from their traditional agricultural economy.

In the organised sector of industry tea plantation occupies a unique position due to its agro-industrial features and the large component of women in the labour force. There has been a continuous decline in the number of working women in most of the organised industries, except tea plantation. Tea plantation is the only industry where the employment of women has not declined in recent years. Rather there has been an increase in the women's employment as compared to men, which clearly indicates that the women are well suited in tea plantation's work. Tea plantation is the only industry where employment has been made on family basis with labourers imported from a distance. This labour recruited from far away places had to be settled down within the confines of the tea plantation. This gave some decisive advantages to the planters. Firstly, a labour force was readily available for plantation as well as for domestic work of the superior staff. Secondly, the labour force could be kept under constant surveillance of the management. And lastly the labour force remaining in semi-isolation would be subjected to little outside influence.

In this general context of tea plantations, the Chandmoni Tea Estate was selected for this study. It represents a typical tea plantation of the Terai and Dooars regions of West Bengal. The composition of labour force, organisation of work and management structure are similar in all the plantations of these two regions. In Chandmoni there are women workers from 19 different Adivasi groups and 2 caste groups. Most of the workers have come from a tribal-peasant background and some are born in Chandmoni or in other tea estates of West Bengal.

The migrant population in this plantation is 36.82 per cent. It constitutes 36.88 per cent of the total Adivasi population. The rest are local born. The women workers were recruited directly or as the bonafide dependents of the men workers.

It has already been mentioned earlier that plantation industry employs more women in proportion to men than in any other organised industry. In the Chandmoni Tea Estate the women constitute 42.91 per cent of the total work force. The causes are : (1) the system of labour recruitment on family basis has made the women also to seek employment obligatorily; (2) plantation work being agro-based the women labourers have a definite function to perform in the industry. As a matter of fact in some type of plantation work, namely, plucking, they are more suited than men; and (3) as the entire labour force is residential the women can take up employment in the plantation without causing serious disruption in their domestic life.

This plantation has also a distinct form of social organisation which gives rise to certain specific form of social relations. Like any other full-fledged industry plantation has an organisation of work and a hierarchy of staff. This hierarchy includes the manager at the top and at the bottom the labour force. The employees can be classified into four categories, namely, managerial staff, staff, sub-staff and workers. Two assistant managers and the doctor are also included along with the manager at the top. Below the managerial category is the staff category which includes the supervisory and clerical staff. In this garden there are 17 such staff, only one of whom is a Bengali woman. In the next sub-staff category there are 55 men who are from Bihari, Nepali and Adivasi communities. None of them are women. Of them 46 are from Adivasis and rest are from the Nepali and Bihari caste groups. The sub-staff draw better pay and facilities than the ordinary workers. The management, so far, has recruited only men in this category. They consider that the nature of work of the sub-staff, being supervisory and to exact work from common workers, is not suitable for the women workers. It was found that the sub-staff are generally promoted from the men workers and this is perhaps the only promotional opportunity for them but even this is denied to the women workers. The women in plantation are to remain throughout their career as daily-rated workers. They are commonly known as 'coolie' or 'aurat'-coolie" The women workers along with their men counterpart, directly involve themselves in the productive system of the plantation. In this sense they, with men workers, are the actual producers in the mode of production of the plantation system who sell their labour to earn a livelihood.

The specific operation in which women are universally engaged is plucking of tea leaf. Men are engaged in agricultural work like hoeing, cleaning the base of the tea bushes, spraying pesticides, etc. They seldom pluck tea-leaf. In slack season women are also employed in light-hoeing and light and medium-pruning. Only young, efficient and able bodied women are employed in such pruning as it needs some skill. In several occupations the women are as efficient as men and in case of plucking of tea leaf women are considered more efficient than men. In peak season the earning of women workers doing plucking on piece-rate basis is higher than that of men. In plantation women are also employed in forking and hoeing and they also do hand weeding. women are not generally employed in tea-factories, only aged and sick women are employed in factory for sweeping and picking out the tea stalks from finished tea. Apart from plucking it was noted that in many other jobs in the plantation women are as efficient as men. Plucking requires patience and dexterity of fingers which the women can provide better than men. The young women workers are also adopted in light pruning and though it requires some skill they can return home as soon as they complete their portion of work on Thika.

Though there is no rigid compartmentalisation of work for male and female workers some sort of division of labour exists. Women are given more manual and relatively unskilled jobs on the ground that they are not "qualified for higher and skilled job" as the management often says.

In this industry there is an obvious discrimination against women in the payment of wages. Their work is always regarded as lighter, and they are often paid at a lower rate. Their working conditions are aggravated by unfair practices that include delay in payment and retention of wage increase, etc.

The difference between wages of men and women workers

still persists. In the early stage of the development of plantation in North Bengal, i.e., before 1950's such wage difference was greater. We find that the Hazri for Thika remained static between 1920 and 1947. It was four annas per Thika for men, three annas for women and one anna and six-pies for children.[1] Gradually after the fixation of minimum wages in 1948 such wage difference was reduced. Upto 1966 there was a difference of 14 paise between the men and women workers. After 1966 the differences rose to 17 paise till the Equal Wages Act was passed in October, 1976. But the employer still refuses to pay equal wages to men and women workers. The women are not regarded as equal to men in their place of work. The Thika for women is less than that of the men workers in plucking and other work. Women are generally given lighter load of work. In case of plucking such Thika for women is 22 kg, whereas it is 25 kg for men, the cultivation work is also 20 per cent lesser and lighter for women than the men workers. A man worker has to perform light pruning of about 60 to 180 tea bushes in a day, whereas a woman worker is alloted only 60 to 100 bushes. In case of weeding and forking a man worker has to weed and fork 160 to 240 bushes, whereas it is about 160 to 200 bushes in case of a female worker.

The management of the plantation feels that the unequal wages between the men and women workers must be maintained as they perform unequal work load. It will be an injustice to the men workers who do most of the heavy work of the plantation. Therefore, the wage differentiation continued upto 1979. In 1982 the planter paid the differences of wages from 1976 retrospectively as the Ministry of labour clarified that the Equal Wages Act applied to the 'equal nature of work,' not to the 'equal volume of work'. But the retention of the increased wages was maintained till July, 1982.

In the plantation hierarchy men have monopolised all the responsible positions. Although in Chandmoni Tea Estate among the daily rated workers women outnumber men and the former are always appointed only as daily-wage workers. They are never appointed to the managerial, executive and administrative positions. The women workers have no promotion facilities.

They cannot even be promoted to the position of Sardars who supervise a group of labourers working in the field. Similarly they cannot be Dafadars, Boidars, Chowkidars, etc. Only a male worker can be promoted to all these positions. By virtue of the occupational statuses the Munshis, Chaprasis, Sardars, Boidars Dafadars, Chowkidars enjoy considerable prestige and privileges in the plantation community. The plantation authority often consults with them. It is found that women workers are always deprived of such honour and privileges. Only during plucking season most of the women workers earn more than that of the men workers as the wages are paid on the basis of the additional quantity of tea leaves plucked. Plucking appears to be the most preferred job for the women workers. On the other hand, plucking appears to be the least preferred job among many of the men workers.

The women workers in the plantation are committed workers in the true sense of the term. The employment in the tea plantation is the only source of their earnings. As the plantation industry is agro-based and is not heavily mechanised the Adivasis and the Nepali caste groups do not face much difficulties to work within the work routine and discipline of the plantation. The traditional agrarian background of the Adivasis and Nepali castes also have helped them to accept plantation works. The field operations in the plantation are very much similar to those of the agriculture. Therefore, the women workers are not strangers to the new environment. They have easily adjusted themselves in the plantation industrial environment which is evident from the low-rate of female absenteeism and rare case of turn over in the industry.

Among the women workers the old and middle aged are more committed than those who are comparatively young. There are several reasons behind it. The young women remain more busy with their household chores and minor children. Those who are comparatively older consider the plantation work as a part of their family activities. On the other hand unmarried women workers are much more committed among all the women workers as they have less family burden. In general, the plantation women workers are committed workers and their loyality is valued more than their efficiency.

It is seen that although some of the men workers have connections with their native villages, in most cases the women workers have cut off their links with their native place. They have gradually established social roots in the plantation. The women workers in plantation appear to be more committed workers than the women in other industries. Though in the plantation system upward mobility in the job among the women workers is nil but job experience to a considerable extent determines the degree of commitment of the women workers. It signifies that despite the absence of upward job mobility commitment of workers in an industry can remain fairly high if the working environment is compatible with the cultural habits and temparament of the workers. Commitment does not necessarily increase with the movement of workers in the occupational hierarchy as has been suggested by some scholars. During the plucking season commitment of the women workers is very high. This is due to their economic interest to earn more wages from plucking extra leaves and also for the nature of the work.

Absenteeism among the men workers is generally due to the social functions and festivals in which they participate and also due to their liquor addiction. Absenteeism among the women workers are due to different reasons. Household work and child rearing activities are the main reasons for absenteeism among the women workers. After receiving weekly wages at least half of the men workers absent themselves from the work for a day or more as they go for a prolonged drinking session. Despite this fact the male workers are less absentees than the women workers. Among the women workers the Ghasis and Baraiks remain more absentee than all other Adivasi and non-Adivasi workers. Without any apparent reason they remain absent from the work. Traditionally the Ghasi were the drummers and musicians and Baraiks were the weavers. It seems that they are ill-suited for the plantation work which is basically agrarian in character. The average rate of absenteeism among the men workers was 20.22 per cent in 1980, whereas it was 24.65 per cent among the women workers in the same year. There are many reasons for women workers' absenteeism. These have been discussed in detail in chapter 4. The major point that emerges from this discussion is that the women workers are burdened with a multitude of domestic work—cultivation of the family patch of land given by the management, cleaning own houses, attending to daily domestic chores, nursing sick children, attending to guests or sometimes visiting friends or relatives in other gardens. There is no relationship between women's involvement in the union and absenteeism because women rarely involve themselves in the union activities.

The job mobility and turnover of men and women workers is very low in the Chandmoni Tea Estate. This is also an indicator of high commitment of the workers. The aspirations of the women workers are low and they do not look for better wages in other industries. Living in the plantation environment with their families they appear to be committed to the plantation industry. Illiteracy has also made them stable wage workers because work in other industries often requires either skill or education.

It was found that, in general, expectations and aspirations of the plantation workers are very low irrespective of age and sex. This is probably due to their traditional cultural background, low economic condition, poor educational level on the one hand and the nature of the industry itself on the other. This, we believe, is further augmented by the settled nature of job in the plantation and the positive encouragement received by the majority of women workers from their families and friends for their job as a worker.

The women workers consider their work as a part of their life. The inclusion of Adivasi women in the work system of the plantation is an important criterion to determine their status whereas the exclusion from all economic and intellectual activities are the criteria of status among the higher caste women. The majority of women who had already worked in a plantation before marriage continue to work after marriage. In many cases the women workers are the primary bread winners. They almost entirely contribute their income to the family expenditure. So economic motivation is central to their work. They seem to be satisfied with their job as they consider it an advantage to earn in a situation of general unemployment. They stoically accept that they will have to maintain their family and children with their income. In this respect their attitudes differ from that of the middle class educated working women. The attitude of the middle class working women is to enjoy some kind of freedom in the society. Sometimes it may also be connected with emancipatory tendency, they try to be economically independent and try to fulfil their life aspiration.[2] But among the plantation women it is a kind of 'enslavement'. They work only to maintain their mere livelihood, family and children.

As has been said above the women workers of plantation work are basically propelled by their economic motivation. Such economic motivation is a result of obligations toward their family and other dependents. The major part of the income goes towards the purchase of daily foods, just as a part of the man's income goes towards the purchase of liquor and tobacco. Some of the families in plantation live in absolute state of misery. They are burdened with non-earning dependents. Family is not considered here as the status unit as in case or urban middle class, but the family in lower class women of plantation is considered as economic unit. It is significant to note that in the eyes of plantation community the working wife enjoys the same amount of prestige as that of her husband.

The plantation owners offer several facilities for them but all these seem to be inadequate. They provide housing, sanitation, dispensary, education, creche, maternity benefits and many other facilities to the workers. The plantation authority has provided these facilities to create a congenial atmosphere for the settlement of family units and in some cases compelled to do so to fulfil legal obligations. However, the health and hospital facilities are inadequate. Previously there was a hospital in the Chandmoni Tea Estate but at present it has been reduced to a illstocked dispensary. The educational level of women workers is very low due to the inadequate educational facilities as well as the general discouraging outlook of the workers towards education. There is no recreational facilities provided for the women workers. There is no organisation for the women workers. There is a creche to keep the infants and children under six years of age, which most mothers do not like to use. Only a few mothers keep their children in the creche as there is no one to look after their children at home.

Most of the women workers come from poor and educationally backward families. Work outside home is not new to them. some of them had worked in the agricultural sector before taking up the plantation work. Work is considered necessary to support the family. The functional role of family has completely changed under the influence of the plantation industry. It has been observed that the structure of the family has undergone remarkable changes. The joint family system has broken down resulting into nuclear families. Traditionally, the agrarian economy required joint living, whereas in the tea industry this system deprives the workers of some of their due benefits from the plantation authority. The plantation provides housing, ration, and other facilities only to the immediate family of a worker. This has obviously helped the nuclearisation of the family structure.

Women workers in other industries face more difficulties at home and in society than at the work place. Work is necessary because without it the family may not survive. But in spite of this material contribution that a woman worker makes to the income of the family, she enjoys no respect or status in the affairs of the family. She is treated more or less like a slave or servant and has to do all the household chores without any help from the husband or other male members. In the society her position is no different.[3]

In the plantation the picture is somewhat different. It was found that most of the women workers are accommodative as their work demands can be fitted into their family requirements. The women workers integrate work and family in their life without any visible strain. Those who cannot integrate the two occasionally absent themselves from work. As the career aspiration of plantation women is very low they tend to pay more attention to their immediate family needs. But normally the work and family both are given more or less equal weightage, so there is less complexity and conflict. Adivasi men help their wives in household work even in cooking and to look after the children. In this respect Adivasi men are more accommodative. This situation has emerged partly due to the traditional tribal ethos of both sexes working for a livelihood.

In the plantation industry work-schedule and working hours help the women adjust with their domestic duties. They can without strain fulfil the roles as wife, mother and a worker. Even if they, sometimes, fail to perform certain household duties their husbands seldom complain. Their children are socialized in such a way with the other children of the community that they never demand more of their mothers' attention. Their friends and relatives never criticise their employment. Increasing emphasis on smaller households, rather than the joint family, makes the husband-wife relationship of crucial importance.

The industrial society normally imposes a strict separation between home and place of work. In tea industry the situation is different. In this industry both the residential and working sectors are within the same area. All these factors seem to have helped the women to adjust better in the plantation work than in any other industry. One evidence to support this contention is that it is only in this industry the rate of employment of women has remained steadily high, if not actually increased, whereas in other industries the rate has fallen down over the past decades.

The women workers, specially the Adivasis suffer from a very few restrictions. They enjoy much more social freedom befitting their traditional tribal ethos. The Nepali caste society is also liberal in this respect. In Adivasi society marriage is simply a contract rather than a sacrament. Though polygyny is permitted, specially in case of barreness of the first wife, monogamy is the general practice. Second marriage after death or divorce of the first wife, is, however, very common.

A boy and a girl can marry according to their own will without prior consent of their parents. Marriage is now a more personal affair than a family one and in the selection of spouse, kinsmen's role has considerably decreased. In many cases, the girl is simply brought and kept in the house permanently. There exists a mutual understanding between the parties, and children born out of such union are socially recognized. No social or ritual ceremonies are performed for this purpose. The plantation society gives provisional recognition to such unions and the families established out of such unions. Inter-ethnic marriages were looked down upon about two decades ago and the couples were driven out of the plantation. But at present such marriages are on the rise and the couples are socially accepted. Such marriage are often settled through the imposition of a fine on the couple by the Adivasi Panchayat or the trade union. Industrial environment provides scope for accommodation of the multi-structural communities. This has increased the inter-actions among the various communities not only in the working place but also in the social life. Due to this reason changes are noticeable in the institution of marriage. Inter-ethnic marriages thus have increased now-a-days. Divorce and remarriage of both men and women are frequent though the trend among the younger couples seems to be declining. One may conclude that family and community's control over the individual of both sexes has become secondary to individual's freedom of action.

The participation of women in plantation work does not adversely affect on inter-personal relationship between husband and wife. It does not create a situation of conflict in the family. However, their husbands and in-laws show positive attitudes towards their employment. Their positive attitude is often equated with their active support.

A high percentage of the husbands show positive attitudes towards their wives' employment. About 98 per cent plantation women state that their husbands want them to work and only 1.8 per cent have said that their husbands are against their working. Almost all women speak of the co-operative attitude of their husbands. These men support their wives' work simply because it brings in money for them and the family. Most of the husbands have mentioned that economic consideration is the main reason for approving the working of their wives. But at the same time they consider women taking up an out-of-home job as something natural in tune with the traditional tribal ethos. The women whose husbands work outside in the railway and in the army and draw better salary are also of the opinion that their wives should continue to work in tea industry since it has been a family occupation for the last two or three generations.

So the economic factor seems to be the primary motive for the women to take up employment in the plantation. Interest in the type of work in plantation is of secondary importance.

In plantation society the domestic and child rearing chores

are not considered below the dignity of men. This is confirmed from the fact that in 71 per cent of the plantation families the husbands extend a helping hand to their wives in housekeeping tasks. Besides sharing of household responsibilities 37.6 per cent of the men workers are of the opinion that their wives should have a say in the important family matters. The rest of the men workers show negative attitudes regarding it but most of these respondents come from the caste groups.

Eightynine per cent of the female workers desire equal participation in decision-making in the family, but in actual practice this is enjoyed only by a few though an almost equal proportion of the women workers hold the view that their role as wage-earners has helped them to raise their status in the society. It is seen that even in vital matters, e.g., children's education, marriage, control of family budget, etc., they play a much lower role than their husbands. As many as 30.77 per cent of the women workers jointly manage the family budget with their husbands. About 41.63 per cent of the women workers do not manage the family budget; their husbands alone control the family budget. Only 23.98 per cent of women workers manage the family budget themselves. Besides, in 3.62 per cent of cases sons or mothers control the family budget. In the case of shopping 64.00 per cent of the women workers do it jointly with their husbands. The rest of the women workers or their husbands do it singly. Most of the husbands spend a large part of the income on liquor and tobacco. However, some of the women workers too have regular drinking habit. Drinking and smoking are not traditionally prohibited among Adivasi men and women. Many of the older women are seen to drink regularly. On festive occasions men and women irrespective of age drink rice-beer. However, women like to take home-brewed rice-beer while men are fond of drinking distilled country-liquor.

The workers' families spend whatever they earn in meeting the basic needs of day to day life. But money available for these needs is substantially depleted due to addiction to drinking. Almost all the families purchase food materials on credit from the grocer's shop and they are burdened with loan. However, among some young women and even some men an organized attempt to give up drinking is noticed. But this is a very recent phenomenon. Three factors seem to have been working behind this change: Conversion to Christianity of a few Adivasi families, education and the influence of caste societies of neighbouring regions and the rising cost of living.

A definite hierarchy exists among the plantation workers which is also reflected in their social life. The members of the cultivating Adivasis (Oraon, Munda, Kheria etc.) consider the members of the non-cultivating Adivasis inferior to them. Hence they never interdine with the latter group. Even the former group consider themselves superior to the Nepali castes groups. They consider the Bengalis and Biharis superior to them in social position. In the case of superior-inferior concept Adivasi women appeared to be more conservative than men. But such social isolation and inter-ethnic barriers are gradually breaking down.

Women workers do join the trade unions but hardly take active part in them. It is not because they are incapable of doing so but because of male dominance in this field. Inequality between men and women has been fully carried over into the trade union organisation. Hardly there is any trade union leader in plantation from among the women workers. Even in the local committees of the trade unions there are a very few women members. Out of 221 women workers of the Chandmoni Tea estate only 10 are active participants. But in a procession or when a demonstration is staged they are placed at the front. From the point of view of women very few of them are also prepared to devote time for regular union activities. As soon as they complete work in the field they rush back to home for attending to their domestic duties. Their husbands also do not like them to keep away from home after their work is over. As a result, the plantation women workers find it extremely difficult to attend union meetings or to visit union office regularly. On most occasions, their membership of union is little more than nominal. As a result, their husbands' discouragement coupled with the pressure of domestic burden have failed to create a working class consciousness and a sense of need to develop a strong trade union movement among them. It was interesting to note that none of the women workers of the plantation even know the name of the trade union to which they belong, whereas at least 60 per cent of the men workers know the names of their respective unions. But at the same time they are used as frontliners whenever a demonstration requires to be staged.

In the Chandmoni Tea Estate the CITU union has its roots deeper among the women workers whereas the RCMC is less popular among them. The women members of the Congress union (RCMC) seldom attend the party meetings. Whereas the CITU women members do take part in party meetings occasionally under the leadership of a Bengali woman. Older women workers are generally supporters of the Congress (RCMC) union but those who are young are much more inclined to the Communist trade union (CITU) membership. However, most of the Christian Oraon women are the Congress union members. They are the oldest settlers of the plantation and the RCMC is also the oldest labour union in this plantation. However, all the women workers, irrespective of their union affiliation are unaware of the ideology of their respective trade unions.

In the plantation the women workers are practically unskilled. They are very poorly educated and organizationally unsophisticated. They themselves are apathetic towards union and politics and avoid conflict with the management so that their wages are regularly paid. Generally they join in strikes and gheraos of the manager and the owner along with the men workers before the Durga Puja in every year demanding increased bonus.

Though there is inter-union rivalry in the Chandmoni Tea Estate particularly among the men workers, it is not so prominent among the women workers. But in a situation of strikes when the women workers are put in front of the management by the agitating mass they become violent. It indicates that they are slowly developing consciousness in participating in the working class movement. However, still the motive for joining the movement remains confined to an immediate benefit of bonus and enhanced wages. This feature is different from that of the advanced industrial society where motive is much wider. Even today the plantation women workers have not yet actively joined the trade union movement due to the lack of lasting class consciousness as they are ignorant of their working condition, discrimination and exploitation.

In the multi-ethnic plantation society the traditional Adivasi council exists alongside with the trade union. The problem of law and order and social control among the workers is managed by the Adivasi Panchayat. The matters settled by these institution are witchcraft, sorcery, inter-ethnic marriage, adultery, theft, inter-ethnic disputes, etc. Traditionally village Panch was represented by the village elders and there was no role of women in such Panchayat. In the present situation in the plantation women workers have also no role in the decision-making process ideally, they can only sit and hear the decisions taken in the Panchayat as silent observers but in practice it is seldom found. As the women have no significant role in the trade union leadership and in the decision-making process in the Panchayat their status in the power structure has not improved. The economic status of the plantation women workers has improved but not in the sense of economic emancipation. But in the power structure their position has remained as low as ever. Their low educational level is also responsible for this low status and they seem to be blissfully unaware of their objective condition.

The educational attainment of the plantation women workers is also very low. In general the level of literacy of the plantation workers is very poor but in case of women it is almost nil. Only 4.5 per cent of the women workers are literate. However, in case of education the sons and daughters are discriminated. Most of the women workers do not want to educate their daughters. They cling to the traditional belief that female education has no use for their employment and for their society. Therefore, the women themselves are more responsible for their educational backwardness than others. The net outcome is that the process of socialization of plantation women promotes a poor self-image of themselves.

It is far from the truth that economic independence has given the plantation women an equal status with men. Though apparently they enjoy considerable freedom, still their overall position in society has remained low. The plantation society is male dominated and women are always treated more or less as a commodity. The inequality between the men and the women extends to almost every sphere of life, in unequal wage rates, unequal occupational status, unequal status in social, political and educational spheres. In the patriarchal plantation society there is no special indentity for women. Identity for equal extent is a far cry. The women are socialized in such a way that social institutions condition them to accept their own exploitation. The patriarchal family system along with the inferior educational standard, economic position and power position of women are the sources of inequality among men and women in the plantation society. It becomes evident that women plantation workers have not witnessed significant changes in their life styles over the years. The social conditions in which they live continue to be traditional having some changes. Their ignorance, lack of skill and assertive nature make them subservient both at the place of work and in the family life.

References

1. Griffiths, P., *History of the Indian Tea Industry,* Weidenfel and Nicolson, London, 1967, p. 310.
2. Mies, M., *Indian Women and Patriarchy,* Concept Publishing Company, New Delhi, 1980.

   Srivastava, V., *Employment of Educated Married Woman in India*, National Publishing House, New Delhi, 1978.

   Kapur, P., *The Changing Status of the Working Woman in India*, Vikas Publishing House, New Delhi, 1974.
3. Karnik, V.B., *Indian Labour-Problems and Prospects,* Minerva Associates (Publications) Pvt. Ltd., Calcutta, 1974, pp. 85-86.

Bibliography

Beteille, A. "The Position of Women in Indian Society" in Devaki Jain (ed.), *Indian Women*, Ministry of Information and Broadcasting, Government of India, New Delhi, 1975.

Bhowmik, S. *Class Formation in the Plantation System*, People's Publishing House, New Delhi, 1981.

"Recruitment Policy of Tea Plantations' in *North-East Quarterly*, Vol. I, No. 2., 1982.

Bista, D.B. *Peoples of Nepal*, Patna Pustak Bhandar, Kathmandu, Nepal, 1980.

Boserup, E. *Woman's Role in Economic Development*, George Allen & Unwin, London, 1970.

Census of India 1961, Vol. I., Monograph No. 11.

Census of India, 1961, West Bengal, District Census Handbook, Darjeeling.

Dalton, E.T. *Tribal History of Eastern India*, Cosmo Publications, New Delhi, 1973.

Dash A.J. Bengal Gazetteers, Darjeeling, 1947.

Desai, N. *Women in Modern India*, Vera & Co. Publishing Private Limited, Bombay, 1957.

D. Souza, V.S."Changing Socio-Economic Conditions and Employment of Women in India" in *Trends of Socio-Economic Changes in India 1871-1961*, Proceedings of a Seminar, Indian Institute of Advanced Study, Simla, 1969.

"Family Status and Female Work Participation" in A. de Souza (ed.), *Women in Contemporary India and South Asia*, Manohar, New Delhi, 1980.

Dube, S.C. "Men's and Women's Role in India" in Barbara E.Ward (ed.), *Women in New Asia,* UNESCO, Paris, 1963.

Engels, F. *The Origin of Family, Private Property and State,* Progress Publishers, Moscow, 1972.

Form, W.H. *Blue-Collar Stratification,* Princeton University Press, Princeton, New Jersey, 1976.

Freeman, J. "The Womens' Liberation Movement in the United States" in R. Rohrlich-Leavitt (ed.), *Women Cross Culturally,* Mouton, Hague, Paris, 1975.

Gadgil, D.R. *Poona. A Socio-Economic Survey,* Gokhale Institute of Politics and Economics, Poona, 1945.

Gait, E. *A History of Assam,* Thacker Spink & Co, Calcutta, 1935.

Goode, W.J. *The Family,* Prentice Hall of India (Pvt) Ltd., New Delhi, 1965.

Griffiths, P. *The History of Indian Tea Industry,* Weidenfel and Nicolson, London, 1967.

Guha, A. *Planter-Raj* to Swaraj, ICHR, New Delhi, 1977.

Gulati, L. "Female Work Participation" in *Economic and Political Weekly,* Vol. X, No 1 and 2, January 11, 1975.

Hamilton, R. *The Liberation of Women,* George Allen and Unwin, London, 1972.

Hate, C.A. *Changing Status of Women in Post-Independence India,* Allied Publishers Private Limited, Bombay, 1969.

Hunter, W.W. *A Statistical Account of Bengal,* Vol. X (Reprinted), D.K. Publishing House, New Delhi, 1974.

I.C.S.S.R. *Status of Women in India,* Allied Publishers Private Limited, New Delhi, 1975.

Indian Labour Gazette, December, 1958.

ILO *Industrial Labour in India,* Series A, Industrial relations, no 41, Geneva, 1938.

ILO *Recent Development of Certain Aspects of Indian Economy - V.* International Labour Office, New Delhi, 1960.

Indian Labour Statistics, 1962.

Indian Labour Statistics, 1971.

Indian Labour Statistics, 1972.

Indian Labour Year Book, 1965.

Jain, D. *Indian Women,* Ministry of Information and Broadcating, Government of India, New Delhi, 1975.

Kapadia, K.M. *Marriage and Family in India,* Oxford University Press, Bombay, 1958.

Kapur, P. *Marriage and Working Women in India,* Vikas Publishing House, New Delhi, 1970.

The Changing Status of Working Women in India, Vikas Publishing House, New Delhi, 1974.

Karnik, V.B. *Indian Labour - Problems and Prospects,* Minerva Associates (Publications) Pvt. Ltd, Calcutta, 1974.

Karve, I. *Kinship Organisation in India,* Asia Publishing House, Bombay, 1965.

Kerr, C., J.T. Dunlop, F.H.Harbison and C.A. Myers *Industrialism and Industrial Man,* Heinemann, London, 1962.

Khanna, G. and M.A. Varghese *Indian Women Today,* Vikas Publishing House, New Delhi, 1978.

Kinzer, N.S. "Socio-cultural Factors Mitigating Role Conflict of Buenos Aires Professional Women" in R. Rohrlich-Leavitt (ed.), *Women Cross Culturally,* Mouton, Hague, Paris, 1975.

Lambert, R.D. *Workers, Factories and Social Change in India,* Princeton University Press, Princeton, N.J., 1963.

Larguia, I. "The Economic Basis of the Status of Women" in R. Rohrlich-Leavitt (ed.), *Women Cross Culturally,* Mouton, Hague, Paris, 1975.

Marx, Karl. *Capital,* Vol. I, Progress Publishers, Moscow, 1971.

Marx, Karl and F. Engels. *The Communist Manifesto,* International Publishers, New York, 1948.

Selected Works, Lawrence and Wishart, London, 1968.

Mead, M. *Male and Female,* Dell Publishing Co, New York, 1948.

Mehotra, G.N. *Studies in Industrial Sociology - The Indian Context,* Atma Ram & Sons, New Delhi, 1975.

Merton, R. *Social Theory and Social Structure,* Free Press, Glencoe, Illĩnoss, 1963.

Middleton, C. "Sexual Inequality and Stratification Theory" in F. Parkin (ed.), *The Social Analysis of Class Structure*, Tavistock Publications, London, 1974.

Mies, M. *Indian Women and Patriarchy*, Concept Publishing Company, New Delhi, 1980.

Millet, K. *Sexual Politics*, Hart Davis, London, 1971.

Mitchill, J. *Women's Estate*, Penguin Books, Harmondsworth, England, 1971.

"Women and Equality" in J. Mitchell and A. Oakley (eds.) *The Rights and Wrongs of Women*, Penguin Books, Harmondsworth, England, 1976.

Mitra, A. *The Status of Women, Literacy and Employment*, ICSSR, Allied Publishers Private Limited, New Delhi, 1979.

Mitra, A., A. Srimany and L.P. Pathak *Status of Women: Household and Non-Household Economic Activity*, ICSSR, Allied Publishers Private Limited, New Delhi, 1979.

Mitra, A., L.P. Pathak and S. Mukherjee, *The Status of Women—Shifts in Occupational Participation 1961-71*, Abhinav Publications, New Delhi, 1980.

Moore, W.E. *Social Change*, Prentice Hall International INC, London, 1963.

Morris, D. Morris "Some Comments in the Supply of Labour to the Bombay Cotton Textile Industry 1854-1951" in *Indian Economic Journal*, 1953, 1 (2).

The Emergence of an Industrial Labour Force: A Study of Bombay Cotton Mills 1854-1947, Berkley, California, 1963.

Morton, F. *The Evolution of Political Society*, Random House, New York, 1967.

Nash, J. "Resistance as Protest: Women in the Struggle of Bolvian Tin-mining communities" in R. Rohrlich-Leavitt (ed.), *Women Cross Culturally*, Mouton, Hague, Paris, 1975.

Nash, M. *Machine Age Maya: The Industrialization in a Guatemalan Community*, American Anthropological Association, Memoir No. 87, 1958.

Nath, K. "Women in the Working Force in India" in *Economic and Political Weekly*, Vol. III, No. 31, August, 3, 1968.

"Urban Women Workers" in *Economic Weekly*, Vol. XVIII, No. 37., September 11, 1965.

Persons, J. *Essays in Sociological Theory*, Light and Life Publishers, New Delhi, 1975.

Piho, V. "Life and Labour of the Women Textile Workers in the Mexico City" in R. Rohrlich-Leavitt (ed.), *Women Cross Culturally*, Mouton, Hague, Paris, 1975.

Ramaswamy, E.A. *The Worker and His Union*, Allied Publishers, New Delhi, 1977.

Ramaswamy, E.A. and Uma. *Industry and Labour*, Oxford University Press, New Delhi, 1981.

Report of the Royal Commission on Labour in India, Government of India, Calcutta, 1931.

Report of Economic and Social Status of Women Workers in India, Labour Bureau, Delhi, 1953.

Report on the Survey of Labour Conditions in Tea Plantations and Tea Factories in India 1961-62, Labour Bureau, Ministry of Labour, Employment and Rehabilitation, Government of India, 1966.

Report of the Central Wage Board for Tea Plantation Industry, Government of India, Delhi, 1966.

Rohrlich-Leavitt, R., B. Sykes, and F. Weatherford "Aboriginal Women: Male and Female Anthropological Perspectives" in R. Rohrlich-Leavitt (ed.), *Women Cross Culturally*, Mouton, Hague, Paris, 1975.

Rowbotham, S. *Woman's Consciousness-Man's World*, Pelican Books, Harmondsworth, England, 1973.

Roy, S.C. *The Oraons of Chota-Nagpur*, The Brahmo Mission Press, Calcutta, 1915.

Sacks, K. "Engels Revisited: Women, the Organization of Production, and Private Property" in R.R. Reiter (ed.), *Towards an Anthropology of Women*, Monthly Review Press, New York, 1975.

Schoepf, B.G. and A.M. Mariotti. "Politics of Theory: Participant Observations in the United States" in R. Rohrlich-Leavitt (ed.), *Women Cross Culturally,* Mouton, Hague, Paris, 1975.

Secombe, W. "Domestic Labour- a Reply to Critics" in *New Left Review,* No. 94, 1975.

Sen, S.N. *The City of Calcutta-A Socio-Economic Survey, 1954-55 to 1957-58* , Book Land Calcutta, 1960.

Sharma, B.R. "Commitment to Industrial Work: The Case of the Indian Automobile Workers" in *Indian Journal of Industrial Relations,* 1968, 4 (1)

The Indian Industrial Worker, Vikas Publishing House Private Limited, New Delhi, 1974.

Sheth, N.R. "The Problem of Labour Commitment" in *Economic and Political Weekly,* 27 February, 1971.

The *Social Framework of an Indian* Factory (2nd edition), Hindustan Publishing Corporation, Delhi, 1981.

Sheth, N.R. and P.J. Patel. *Industrial Sociology in India,* Rawat Publications, Jaipur, 1970.

Singh, A.M. "The Study of Women in India: Some Problems in Methodology" in A. de Souza (ed.), *Women in Contemporary India*, Manohar, New Delhi, 1975.

"The Study of Woman in South Asia: Some Current Methodological and Research Issues" in A. de Souza (ed.), *Women in Contemporary India and South Asia,* Manohar, New Delhi, 1980.

Sinha, D. "Control of Industrial Absenteeism" in *Indian Journal of Labour Economics,* Vol. IV, No. 2, July 1961.

Sinha, J.N. "The Indian Working Force: Its Growth and Changing Composition" in *Census of India,* 1961, Vol. I, Monograph No. 11, Office of the Registrar General India, Ministry of Home Affairs, New Delhi, 1972.

Silvestrini-Pacheco, B. "Women as Workers: The Experience of the Puerto Rican Woman in 1930's" in R. Rohrlich Leavitt (ed.), *Women Cross Culturally,* Mouton, Hague, Paris, 1975.

Srinivas, M.N. *The Changing Position of Indian Women,* Oxford University Press, New Delhi, 1978.

Srivastava, V. *Employment of Educated Married Women in*

India, National Publishing House, New Delhi, 1978.

Tea Statistics Tea Board of India, Calcutta, 1957.

Tea Statistics Tea Board of India, Calcutta, 1959.

Tea Statistics Tea Board of India, Calcutta, 1968-69.

Tea Statistics Tea Board of India, Calcutta, 1969-70.

Tea Statistics Tea Board of India, Calcutta, 1976.

Tea Statistics Tea Board of India, Calcutta, 1977-78.

Tea Statistics Tea Board of India, Calcutta, 1978-79.

Tea Statistics Tea Board of India, Calcutta, 1981-82.

Thorner, D. "Casual Employment of a Factory Labour Force: The Case of 1850-1939" in *Economic Weekly*, 1957, Annual number.

Index